RUTH & ESTHER

Women of the Providence of God

RUTH & ESTHER

Women of the Providence of God

Walter C. Kaiser, Jr.

Lederer Books
An imprint of
Messianic Jewish Publishers
Clarksville, MD 21029

Published by:

Lederer Books

An imprint of Messianic Jewish Publishers

6120 Day Long Lane

Clarksville, MD 21029

Distributed by:

Messianic Jewish Publishers & Resources

Order line: (800) 410-7367 lederer@messianicjewish.net

www.MessianicJewish.net

Dedicated To
My Eight Lovely Step Great-Grandaughters:

Moriah Faith Stecker	Ellyana Grace Murphy
Selah Marie Stecker	Jaydalyn Hope Murphy
Norah Grace Stecker	Aniyah Joy Murphy
Kinley Sue Stecker	Harlow Brave Stecker

Table of Contents

RUTH
A Woman of Valor

ESTHER
A Girl with Both Inner and Outer Beauty

RUTH

A Woman of Valor

Lesson 1

Introduction to the Book of Ruth

A Beautiful Book

Almost all writers, regardless of theological positions, give high praise to the book of Ruth. For example, Alexander Schroeder enthused, "No poet in the world has written a more beautiful short story." Goethe called Ruth "the loveliest compete work on a small scale handed down to us as an ethical treatise."[1] Another author warned, "So delicate in its transparent simplicity [is this book] that the worse service one can do to the story is to comment on it."[2] This sample of opinions speaks of how highly the book is regarded, even in the broad culture.

A Book Featuring a Non-Israelite

It is surprising that a book in Scripture features and praises a non-Israelite, not to mention that from the loins of this woman would come in her ancestral line one who would be the Savior of the World. But the book has additional reasons for being recognized as outstanding.

Ruth herself only speaks 120 words in ten speeches. It is unusual for the one for whom the book is named to say less than anyone else. (The book has 85 verses and 1294 words.[3]) In fact, by frequency, it could have been called "Naomi" or "Boaz," who speak 225 words in 12 speeches and

---

1. Both quoted in A. Weiser, *Introduction to the Old Testament*, 305.

2. Richard Moulton, *The Modern Reader's Bible*, in Cyril Barber, *A Story of God's Grace: Ruth*, 139.

3. For these figures, see Daniel Block, *The New American Commentary: Judges and Ruth*, 588, n. 5.

281 words in 14 speeches, respectively. Or what about little "Obed," the person toward whom the whole narrative is moving? He was the scion from the line of the coming King David!

When all is said and done, despite all these numbers, even more remarkable is that Ruth is the only non-Israelite for whom a book of the Bible is named. Ruth is both a foreigner and an immigrant, a fact the writer never lets us forget; five times he says, "Ruth the Moabitess" (vv. 1:22; 2:2, 21; 4:5, 10), not "Ruth the Israelite." But this fact is also one of the great points of this book: God's grace and love reaches out to all, even to the hostile adversaries of Israel, such as the (gentile) Moabites.

A Book of Conversations

It is unusual for the writer of a biblical book to build the whole story around a series of conversations, brief as they are, taken from the main characters. Of the 85 verses in the book, 55 of those verses record its conversations. Of the 1294 words in the book, 678 (or 52.4%) come from the lips of the main characters. True, the Old Testament narrative rarely uses characterization to depict its story, but it does use an abundance of dialogue with minimal intervention by the narrator to inform us as to what is going on in the narrative. Even more striking is the fact that often the narrator of a story in the Old Testament will allow the leading person in that story to make the key statement and the point on which the whole episode rests.

The Doctrine of the Providence of God

The great outcry that emerges from the opening crisis of the book of Ruth is: "Where are you, God of the universe, when we face such enormous trouble?" In many ways, such a cry is similar to those that come in our own times, for we who believe in the God who created this universe also believe he not only rules this world but also sustains it and thus is available for all who find themselves in grief, disaster, pain and harm's way. This is what Scripture calls the "Doctrine of Providence."

If providence is the name we give to the present work of our Lord in his present activity in this world, it is to be distinguished from his creative work in creation, by which he brought everything into existence. But this is a separate work from his sustaining work in which all life and breath continuously depend on the Lord for all of our existence. It should not be thought unrealistic, therefore, that a Creator God should use order and causality in this world to make things happen. No, he will not act outside of what he is in his being and what he can do in his works. He will uphold the very order he has created despite the changes and nuances of the times, for this is why we have come to expect God to steer and guide all the natural world, the world of mortals, and the history of nations. In summary, then, "Providence" is the gracious outworking of God's sovereignty, one in which all events are directed, permitted or disposed by him, to work out his will and his plan for all this world and all its times.

It is important to distinguish between God's "general providence" and "special providence." In general providence, God shows his power over the universe through his use of general rules that operate according to the created rules of nature, without needing special acts of direct divine intervention of his will in every case. In God's "special providence," he manifests his working in direct response to special situations or persons using aspects of his work usually not seen in the laws of creation. It is his special providence, therefore, that we see operating in the book of Ruth. Such acts must not be confused with what we call a "miracle," which is a unique work of God done to vindicate either his message or his messenger of the Gospel. Such miracles attest to the messenger's heavenly credentials.

The Divine Purpose in the Book of Ruth

Locating the divine purpose and reason for our Lord giving us the book of Ruth is not as difficult as some make it seem. Ronald Hals[4] brilliantly shows that Ruth wants us to see God's hand in what might

---

4. Ronald M. Hals, *The Theology of the Book of Ruth*.

otherwise seem to be a series of coincidences or natural, ordinary events. We are shown how God is directly involved in all of life without experiencing the interrupting presence of the narrator to explain that this is what is happening in these events.

The hand of the Lord can be seen, for instance, in the famine that begins the book. It is not as if this would have been unexpected, for God had warned (Lev. 26:19–20, Deut. 28:23–24) that this was exactly what would happen if his people rejected his teaching and his right to be Lord of their lives. So often in this book, what looks like an accident, or a chance occurrence was an example of God's special providence. In this way, the author of Ruth underplayed some events for the sake of effect. Often what was veiled was nothing less than the active hand of God, even in the minute details of life. An example of this would be Ruth 3:8. Even as the book closes, God's hand could also be seen once more even in the legal processes of v. 4:1–12.

The Book's References to God

To learn the theology of a book of the Bible, we need only ask what a writer says (or even implies) about God. It is striking that the book of Ruth mentions God 23 times, with only two of those instances coming from the narrator (vv. 1:6; 4:13). All the other references come from the lips of the characters in this narrative. The covenantal name for God, usually rendered in English as "LORD" (YHVH) appears 17 times and is reserved in Scripture to be used exclusively by those who have a personal relationship with him, and who are living under his covenant. The general name for God in Hebrew is Elohim, rendered in English as "God," which appears four times, one time of which is a name for Chemosh, the god of the Moabites. The most unusual name for God in this book is Shaddai, an ancient name for God, used in the books of Job and Genesis, meaning something like "the One Nourishing" or the "God of the Mountain."

However, the most frequent use of God's name in this book is in times of prayer, where it appears nine times. Even the greetings in the book are all prayers of blessing in the name of the Lord. Every one of the major characters in the book is the object of a prayer, and each prayer is answered. All these references to God reinforce the fact that Ruth is a story about God's providence and a clear assertion of his sovereignty. Nowhere is this brought out more definitely than in the ending given to this narrative, v. 4:11–14; in that description a child is born who is a gift from the Lord himself. Despite the book's lack of any words like "divine providence," God's providential hand shines through every line of this story, as it draws our attention to the intervention of God in the everyday affairs of life.

The Setting, Time, and Background of the Book of Ruth

The setting is clearly given in the opening verse, "In the days when the Judges ruled, there was a famine in the land." Moreover, the concluding genealogies of the book take us all the way up to the time of King David around 1000 B.C.E. That a famine had been permitted in the providence of God during the lifetime of this family alerts us to the fact that something is spiritually wrong in Israel, for the Lord is calling for repentance and a change in the loyalty the people give to him! It is the love of God that moves us to action by the sudden absences of what we had previously come to count on as always being present.

This adversity comes when a man from Bethlehem of Judah, named Elimelekh, left Israel with his wife Naomi and his two sons, Mahlon and Kilion, to go to live in Moab, while the famine lasted in Israel (v. 2). Moab was a nation to the east of Israel and situated on a narrow strip of cultivatable land on a rather high plateau some 3300 feet above sea level. This land was bounded on the west by a sharp escarpment, which dropped down to the Dead Sea at 1300 feet below sea level. On the east it was bordered by the high desert; on the north, it was marked off by the Jabbok River. Its southern border was set off by what is called today, *Wadi al Hesa*, likely the same as the ancient Zered River.

The origins of the people of Moab, unfortunately, were not at all noble, even though they could be traced to the family of Abraham in Genesis 12, 13, 19. Abraham's nephew, Lot, left Ur of the Chaldees (modern Iraq) with Abraham. To avoid conflict over grazing rights, for both Lot and Abraham had large herds and flocks, Abraham gave Lot his choice of land. Lot chose the most fertile and best-watered land in the Plain of Jordan, where Sodom and Gomorrah, two of the five cities in that plain, were situated. Later, when the five cities of the Jordan Plain were invaded by four kings from Mesopotamia, they captured Lot, his family and all their herds and goods and carted them off as captives. Abraham, however, strengthened in might by the awesome hand of God, took his 318 servants and overpowered the four kings in a surprise night raid on the four kings at the northern city of Dan.

Later, Lot, his wife and two daughters were told to flee Sodom before it and Gomorrah were destroyed. Lot's wife was lost by disobedience, so she suffered the judgment of God; she turned around to see the destruction of the cities and was turned into a pillar of salt. Subsequently, Lot's two daughters dreamed up a plan to get their father drunk and conceive children by him. His older daughter had a son named Moab, and his younger daughter had a son named Ammon. Thus, we have the incestuous roots of the nations of Moab and Ammon.

Ruth in the Dead Sea Scrolls and Order of Books in the Bible

Ruth is well-preserved in four fragments of the Dead Sea Scrolls, which attests to its accuracy. In a rare case of agreement, all scholars and readers of Ruth agree it should be included among the authoritative books given us by God. There is some small disagreement, however, on the placement in the order of the books of the Bible. Our English versions follow the order in the Greek Septuagint Bibles, which place Ruth right after Judges, to position it in as close to its historical and chronological context; in the days of Gideon, in Judges, a famine seemed to occur.

In most Hebrew versions of Ruth, this book is placed near Proverbs. No doubt this is because Ruth is seen as a beautiful example of the "Noble [Virtuous] Woman" (*Eshet Chayil*) mentioned in the poem dedicated to that woman in Proverbs 31:10 (see Ruth 3:11). In a very few manuscripts in the Jewish tradition, Ruth is placed just before Psalms, perhaps to give recognition to King David's origins and his work of composing half of the 150. A good case can be made for any one of these three locations for the placement of Ruth in the canon of Scripture.

Outline for the Book of Ruth

Ruth can best be appreciated for all its literary qualities by being read in its entirety in one sitting. God's beautiful work of providence emerges as one reads the story with an eye to both the direct and indirect references to God. Even though his providence is sometimes veiled or even hidden, the point is that God is still present, and the book therefore forms a defense for the fact that his hand is never far away from the events of our everyday experiences, even though we cannot always see it operating or its presence!

The Plan and Outline Suggested in the Book of Ruth

Lesson 2: God's Providence in Times of Adversity – Ruth 1:1–22

Lesson 3: In the Coincidences Found in Our Lives – Ruth 2:1–23

Lesson 4: In the Risky Schemes We Take in Our Lives – Ruth 3:1–18

Lesson 5: In the Surprising Outcomes of Our Lives – Ruth 4:1–22

Conclusions

1. God is the One we can count on when we think we are in the most serious difficulties and most painful events in our lives.

2. God gives special care to families, for he is the One who has given to us the gift of families and has built families as the base for all society.

3. God has providentially provided for us to learn many lessons in life by sensing that even if his working for us is veiled, it still is his gift to all who trust him.

4. God has placed a special story about a key woman to encourage all women that he loves them and has special plans for them as well, as he has for the men.

Lesson 2

God's Providence in Times of Adversity

Ruth 1:1–22

Elimelekh's Family Leaves Bethlehem Only to Go from Famine to Facing Death

The book of Ruth is set in the days of the Judges, in the very days when the Midianites would annually invade Israel; they would steal the produce of the land just as the crops were maturing (Judg. 6:1–6). Apparently, Elimelekh (which means "My God and King") and his wife Naomi ("sweet, pleasant") had had enough of such piracy and hiding in caves to save their lives, so they decided to leave Bethlehem and move to Moab, a land that worshiped the god Chemosh, just east and on the other side of the Dead Sea. Soon after moving, Elimelekh died, and Naomi was left with the two boys. This couple had gone with their two sons, *Mahlon* ("sickness") and *Kilion* ("destruction"), but both also soon died, so again Naomi was left by herself. The meaning of the boys' names is enough to tell the story of those years of exile, for they did face "sickness and destruction," if not death itself. All these personal names are attested in the archaeological finds of Ugaritic (a language that shares 60% of its vocabulary with Hebrew), adding another note to the historicity of this book.

This exiled remnant of a family of four was now reduced to just one woman, for at that point the text says she "was left." However, the boys had married in the interim two Moabite women, Orpah and Ruth. That too presented another spiritual problem, for Deuteronomy 23:3–4 forbade any children of the Moabites from participating in Israel's religious life. The reason for this injunction was because they refused to offer any help to

Israel with food and water when they wanted to pass through their land as Israel wandered through the wilderness!

Naomi Hears the Lord Has Come to the Aid of His People Back Home – 1:6–14

With Elimelekh gone, Naomi must take over as the leader of the family. The Lord had "visited" (*paqad*) his people by making food available for them as he promised in his covenant. Moreover, using this same verb of "visiting," he will "give" conception to Ruth (4:13); these two verbs formed as it were an inclusion for this text. Thus, in verse 6 Naomi is told to "arise" (*wattaqam*) and return to the land they had left in Bethlehem. With this action, the Lord now will use her to direct the course of this family, which will lead to Israel's redemption.

At first, both Orpah and Ruth, the newly arrived daughters-in-law, are willing to leave their native Moab after both their husbands die (vv. 6–7), but Naomi was apprehensive about these women making such a move, so she adamantly opposed their returning with her to Israel. So, she urged both Orpah and Ruth to go back home to their mother's house (v. 8). In so doing, Naomi did however, invoke a blessing on the girls as her parting gift as she declared:

> "May the LORD show kindness (*hesed*) to you, as you have shown to your dead and to me. May the LORD grant that each of you will find rest (*menuhah*) in the home of another husband." (1:8b–9a)

It is most interesting that Naomi invoked the covenantal name of God as she blessed both women. Obviously, she must have shared with both daughters-in-law the teaching about the Lord God of Israel and his saving grace he offered them. Naomi did not try to be culturally correct by appealing to the Moabite national deity Chemosh; she forthrightly gave her blessing in the name of the Lord her God! Moreover, she asked the God of the universe to show both of these women his loyal love, mercy, and loving kindness.

This was a most emotional scene for the women, for the prospect of their permanently parting in light of the tragedy that had befallen them caused them to weep aloud as they kissed each other in deep affection, for they by now decided: "We will go back with you to your people" (v. 10). They could not bear the thought of being forever separated from Naomi. This speaks well of both Naomi and the character of the women from Moab. These women must have had quite a good working relationship, despite the deaths that had intruded into their lives. Surely that speaks volumes in favor of the view that Naomi must have been remarkably close and a wonderful example to these ladies.

However, Naomi firmly renounced both ladies' resolve to go back to Judah with her, for it just went beyond any good common sense. Why would the two continue traveling back to Israel with her? Surely Naomi did not think she was going to have any more newborn sons, and even if she was so fortunate, would these women wait until they had matured and had grown up enough to marry them? Would the ladies remain unmarried and wait for the prospect of newborn sons from Naomi's womb? (vv. 11–13) Anyway, Naomi herself was already too old to remarry.

Naomi decided that such a long wait was out of the question. In her view, her name no longer meant "pleasant" or "sweetness." Her name now would be *Mara*, meaning "bitter." Clearly, she argued, God's hand had gone out against her. Her story had become like that of Job's; even though at the same time she had invoked God himself to bless her two daughters-in-law, Naomi blamed God for the famine and the death of her husband and sons. The women once more broke out in deep crying and sadness. Life was filled with deep sorrow and suffering.

Ruth the Moabite Pledges Her Loyalty to Naomi and to Her God – 1:15–19a

Orpah acted on her decision to follow the directions Naomi had just given, so she returned home to reintegrate herself into Moabite society, but for Ruth, this was a whole other story. Orpah returned not only to her mother's house, as Naomi suggested, but to her Moabite people and to the gods of that land (v. 15)!

But Ruth would not let Naomi convince her to return to her mother's home, her people, and the gods of that land (v. 16). Her pledge was entirely different from Orpah's. Ruth solemnly requested and pledged:

> "Don't urge me to leave you or to turn back from you. Where you go, I will go, and where you stay, I will stay. Your people will be my people and your LORD my God. Where you die, I will die, and there I will be buried. May the LORD deal with me, be it ever so severely, if anything but death separates you and me." (1:16–17)

With the seriousness and the solemnity of that affirmation, Naomi could plainly see that Ruth was determined to go back to Bethlehem with her, so she no longer urged her to act otherwise. Thus, the two women journeyed on until they came to the land of Judah.

Naomi Arrives Back in Bethlehem, Startling Her Former Neighbors – 1:19b–22

Women continue to play the key role in this story. When Naomi's former neighbors saw her, the whole town "was aroused" (Hebrew *hum*, denoting a loud ringing), asking one another, "Is this Naomi?" (v. 19b). She was quick to answer that the town could forget about her old name, "sweetness" (*naomi*), which they had known her by in former days, for her name now, self-assigned based on the tragedies she had experienced, was now *mara*, "bitter" (v. 20). The reason she had assumed this new designation was

> "The Almighty (Shaddai) has made my life bitter. I went away full, but the Lord has brought me back empty. Why do you call me Naomi? The Lord has afflicted me; the Almighty has brought misfortune upon me." (1:20–21)

Naomi has no explanation as to why the Lord has harmed her, for she has interpreted his actions against her as the result of personal sin. She seems to ask of herself: "Should Elimelekh and I have stayed in Bethlehem, just as our neighbors had done?" That is the implied question that lies just at the edge of her thinking.

Thus, it was that Naomi had left the foreign land of Moab after a decade of living through tragedies in that land, for now she was coming back home to Judah accompanied by "Ruth the Moabitess," a designation that appears five times in this book (v. 2). It is as if she questioned: "What good will my bringing back a Moabitess do for Bethlehem?" But God was not finished with Naomi or Ruth; the story was far from over!

Conclusions

1. If Rahab, a Canaanite, was received as a member of the family of God in Israel (Josh. 2:9–13), should we have any hesitancies about doing the same for Ruth the Moabitess? In fact, this story will go far beyond the fact that Ruth's soon-to-be-born son will be in the line of Messiah!

2. Was Naomi correct in her assumption that the trials that had been introduced into her life happened because of some known sin in her life, or did she make that up?

3. Did the Lord authorize Elimelekh's going into exile into Moab to avoid the famine in the land? If not, then why did God see fit to use Ruth in the Messianic line of David and Yeshua? Or can God operate despite human circumstances?

4. What role do you think the neighbors of Elimelekh and Naomi might have played as they welcomed their former friends home?

5. God's ways and works are not always immediately obvious to us, but he calls us to trust him, even when things look desperate, for he is still at work and carrying out his plans.

Questions for Thought and Reflection

1. In your opinion, do the annual invasions of the Midianites to steal the crops from Judah seem to be the reason and time when there was a famine in the land that cause this couple to leave Judah?

2. Why do you think Ruth followed Naomi back to her country, but Orpah chose not to? What was the difference between the two of them?

3. Were the sons of this couple acting on biblical grounds when they married the two women from Moab? How did Ruth's marrying a relative of the family fit into God's plan?

4. What do you think motivated Ruth to make such a strong affirmation in her choosing to go back to Judah with Naomi, including being a part of her people and her God?

5. Was Naomi justified in declaring that the Almighty, the Lord God, had made her life bitter and harsh? Why did she use the distinctive older name of Shaddai for God?

Lesson 3

Ruth Gleans Barley in the Fields of a Family Relative Named Boaz

Ruth 2:1–23

Suddenly we are introduced to a relative of Naomi's husband Elimelekh, a "man of standing," named Boaz, meaning "strength is in him." Boaz was well situated in life, for he is called a "strong warrior" (3:14). Also, in the Hebrew order of the canon, Ruth is preceded by Proverbs, which ends with an alphabetic acrostic with the same title as is given to Ruth in Proverbs 31:10–31, "a woman of *hayil*." Moreover, in Ruth 4:11, the Lord is petitioned to bless the marriage of Ruth and Boaz with might and strength (*hayil*). Therefore, this Hebrew term highlights a central characteristic of both Boaz and Ruth: They both were persons of inner strength and determination.

Ruth Gleans in Boaz's Barley Fields – 2:17

Five times, Ruth is labeled "the Moabitess" (v. 2:2). Now that the narrative has introduced us to Boaz and his relationship to Elimelekh, it picks up again by describing how it was that Ruth met Boaz. It all began with Ruth asking her mother-in-law Naomi for permission to join the impoverished gleaners of the land who were picking up the grain that had been dropped as leftovers or missed stalks with the grains of barley that the laborers had unintentionally passed by. Ruth asked to go into whatever field she might find favor from the landowner in this season of the barley harvest.

All such gleaning was in accord with the Torah; Deuteronomy 24:19–20 and Leviticus 19:9–10 specifically provided for such activity:

> When you are harvesting in your field and you overlook a sheaf, do not go back to get it. Leave it for the alien, the fatherless and the widow, so that the LORD your God may bless you in all the work of your hands. When you beat olives from your trees, do not go over the branches a second time. Leave what remains for the alien, the fatherless and the widow. (Deut. 24:19–20)

> When you reap the harvest of your land, do not reap to the very edges of your field or gather the gleanings of your harvest. Do not go over your vineyard a second time or pick up the grapes that have fallen. Leave them for the poor and the alien. I am the LORD your God. (Lev. 19:9–10)

Naomi gave Ruth permission to go harvest food for both of them with the words "Go ahead my daughter," so Ruth went and chose a field where some gleaners were already harvesting what had been left over by the workers in the field. However, most amazing of all, the field she happened to choose belonged to Boaz, whom the narrator already told us was a relative through her deceased father-in-law Elimelekh (v. 2:3). The Hebrew word here, *qarah*, is translated "as it turned out" by the NIV, but not with the connotation of, "As luck would have it." There is no room in the Bible for chance, luck, or random happenings. Ruth's choice of field was, in fact, guided by the providential hand of God. Luck had nothing to do with it; it was the strong intervention of God leading Ruth every step in the way!

There is more evidence for providence in this story, for just at that time Boaz, the relative and owner of the field, arrived from Bethlehem and greeted the harvesters, saying "The LORD be with you!" (v. 2:4) They, of course, gave the traditional response, "The LORD bless you!" His first word to his workers was a word about his God and his blessing.

Suddenly Boaz must have noticed a newcomer among the gleaners, for he asked his foreman on the job, "Whose young woman is that?" Being young, she must have stood out among those who were widows and older persons. The foreman knew the answer:

"She is the Moabitess who came back from Moab with Naomi. She said, 'Please let me glean and gather among the sheaves behind the harvesters.' She went into the field and has worked steadily from morning till now, except for a short rest in the shelter." (2:6–7)

Ruth and Boaz had not met up to this point, for he had just been introduced by Boaz's foreman. The Hebrew word here translated "foreman" is *na'ar*, meaning literally a "young man."

Ruth and Boaz Have Their First Meeting – 2:8–13

There is a sudden transition from the overseer's identification of this stranger and a lively conversation between the landowner and the newly arrived young woman from Moab (v. 2:8ff). Boaz addressed her in a fatherly way:

"My daughter, listen to me. Don't go and glean in another field and don't go away from here. Stay here with my servant girls. Watch the field where the men are harvesting and follow along after the girls. I have told the men not to touch you. And whenever you are thirsty, go and get a drink from the water jars the men have filled." (2:8–9)

Boaz promised Ruth she would be most satisfied and safe in gleaning in his fields. He told her he had warned his young men not to "touch" her (*naga'*), a word with sexual connotations, such as touching or molesting. Moreover, Boaz invited Ruth to satisfy her thirst by drinking from the supply or well he had made available in the shelter. Some interpreters think Boaz is also alluding to the allegorical meaning of Proverbs 5:15–19, "Drink water from your own cistern, flowing water from your own well. …Rejoice in the wife of your youth.…Be captivated always with her love." But this seems a stretch, for there is no reference here to a well or a cistern in this shelter.

With such kind words coming from an almost total stranger, Ruth "bowed down with her face to the ground and asked, "Why have I found such favor in your eyes that you notice me—a foreigner?" (2:10). Her "bowing down" seems at first an exaggerated display of gratitude, but perhaps if we had known Ruth, we would have thought it altogether in character. Ruth is overwhelmed by this landowner's graciousness, especially since she is a foreigner. In fact, there may be a little pun involved in Ruth's speech, for the word "to take notice," *nakar*, uses the same triconsonantal Hebrew root as the word for "foreigner" or "alien," *nokri*. Ruth's humility and beautiful response surely moved the heart of Boaz.

Boaz was moved to respond back to Ruth's gracious attitude:

> "I've been told about what you have done for your mother-in-law since the death of your husband—how you left your father and mother and your homeland and came to live with a people you did not know before. May the LORD repay you for what you have done. May you be richly rewarded by the LORD, the God of Israel, under whose wings you have come to take refuge." (2:11–12)

Naomi and Ruth had arrived just in time to get in on the barley harvest, so she had had little, if any, time for leisure or welcoming teas with the ladies of the village. Boaz concluded his speech by promising that the Ruth will earn wages from the Lord as a payment for her unusual acts of kindness in accompanying her mother-in-law, Naomi.

Boaz Invites Ruth to Eat with Him and the Harvesters – 2:14–17

It is becoming quite clear that Boaz is very affected by Ruth, who has a lot of characteristics he likes. Were the harvesters noticing some of the same hints that were going on between their boss and this foreigner. She was an extraordinary woman! No wonder Boaz took a personal interest in her. No wonder, then, that he invited Ruth, "Come over here. Have some bread and dip it in the wine vinegar!" (2:14)

As Ruth sat down with the harvesters, Boaz "offered her some roasted grain." Eventually she had more than her fill, for she had some of her meal left over, which she would later take home to share with Naomi. However, when the meal was over, she promptly made her way back into the fields to do some more gleaning. In the meantime, Boaz had given orders to his men: "Even if she gathers among the sheaves, don't embarrass her. Rather pull out some stalks for her from the bundles, don't embarrass her" (2:15–16). One can almost imagine a few hushed chuckles that seemed to say, "The boss must really be sweet on this girl!"

So, Ruth continued to glean in the field until evening (v. 2:17). She is sounding increasingly like that "woman of valor" (*'ashet hayil*) described in Proverbs 31:10–31.

Naomi Names Boaz as Their Kinsman-Redeemer – 2:18–23

Ruth lugged back to the town of Bethlehem what she had gathered that day—an ephah of grain, weighing between 20 and 50 pounds. So startled was Naomi by the enormous amount Ruth had gathered that day that she asked: "Where did you glean today? Where did you work?" The first "where," *epho*, is connected in Hebrew as a pun on *ephah*. The second "where" is a different Hebrew word.

Ruth told Naomi the name of the man in whose fields she had been working all day. When she revealed his name was Boaz (v. 2:19b), Naomi's whole countenance and view on life changed radically, for Naomi almost shouted: "That man is our close relative; he is one of our kinsman-redeemers!" (v. 20) With that statement, we have reached the heart and the focal point of this chapter and the book itself!

Boaz became the means God used to show Naomi his goodness, for it is impossible to separate God from his agent Boaz in Naomi's words: "May he be blessed by the LORD who has not forsaken his *hesed* (grace)."

Was the antecedent of Boaz, or the Lord? (v. 2:20) Naomi's bitterness over her circumstances had so hardened her moods under what she had by then deemed nothing less than a sign of God's judgment that she was beginning to be hard to deal with. But this news of Ruth's coming upon Boaz's field and receiving his lavish kindness was now a contrary message as to how she thought God was dealing with her.

Through Boaz's graciousness to Ruth, Naomi was now coming to see that the Lord had not stopped showing his covenantal mercies and faithfulness to her. This work of grace came, of course, from our Lord, "whose kindness has not forsaken the living [plural in number] and the dead." The word "living" had the meaning of both Naomi and Ruth as well as the family of Elimelekh. Here, also, is the first occasion that Ruth is spoken of as being included in the family of Naomi.

The concept of a kinsman-redeemer is very interesting. This person was obligated under the law (Lev. 25:25–55) to repay his relatives if one of them fell into debt and had to sell himself into debt slavery. Likewise, the kinsman-redeemer was obligated to marry the widow in the family and to raise up a child for his brother who had died childless (Deut. 25:5–10). By doing so, the inheritance of the land would continue in the name and family of the man who had died.

All this was true, but the case of Ruth did not seem to meet the Torah's legal requirements, as Boaz was not a direct brother to Elimelekh. Thus, describing Boaz as a kinsman-redeemer who had some sort of legal obligation to Naomi does not seem correct! Moreover, the law did not address the issue of foreigners who legally had been married into the family. So, the question remained: Did the kinsman-redeemer have a legal obligation to Naomi or Ruth? If Boaz wanted to use any loopholes in the law to avoid obligation to the family of Elimelekh there were plenty of opportunities to avoid responsibility.

However, Boaz was a greater man than one who only went by the letter of the law, for he had been touched in his heart by the Lord Almighty. He also was a man who took seriously his covenantal responsibilities. This is a hard word to translate into English, for it entails many different things such as love, grace, mercy, and kindness.

But there is something more important here, for referring to Boaz as a kinsman-redeemer points beyond him to the real Redeemer, the Lord! We have seen the grammatical difficulty of whether the text meant it was Boaz or the Lord who showed mercy to Ruth and Naomi. The conclusion was that Boaz was the means God used to help Naomi get past her bitterness about what she perceived were the lashes of God's judgment. But then Naomi realized God had not stopped showing his covenant faithfulness to her and Ruth.

Naomi counseled Ruth not to desert Boaz's fields but to stay with his laborers, for if she went to some of the fields of other owners, she might come to some harm (v. 2:22). Boaz had acted as a kinsman-redeemer by supplying Naomi and Ruth food to eat, but did he think it was his duty to give them an offspring as well? If he had been willing to meet one need of these two ladies, perhaps he might be willing to meet the other need as well.

Meanwhile, Ruth's biological clock continued to tick away. Naomi and Ruth had arrived home at the beginning of the barley harvest (v. 1:27), just in time for celebrating the Passover when the grain harvest was begun (Deut. 16:9). But now that the barley harvest had ended, some seven weeks had passed, which meant they were now up to the Feast of Firstfruits, the Festival of Weeks, also called Pentecost. Boaz had helped the women to see the fruits and the blessing of God's grace in the gifts of grain he had given them. But Pentecost was the day God would choose to pour out his Spirit on Jews and Gentiles alike, as they were immersed into one body and made to drink one drink (Acts 2:1–39; 1 Cor. 12:12–13).

So, Ruth stayed with Boaz's servant girls gleaning both the barley and then the wheat harvest until they were completed. Ruth continued to live with her mother-in-law Naomi (v. 2:23b).

Conclusions

1. The word *hesed* is used to describe Boaz as an outstanding man of great generosity and kindness, even to foreigners.

2. Ruth is five times labeled in this book as "the Moabitess." But she is a hard worker who continues the job all day long, for she was not looking for a free handout.

3. When Boaz met her, he was so impressed by her that he urged her to stay in his fields with the servant girls collecting missed grains left behind by his laborers. Boaz had further instructed his men not to touch her and also to give her water from the jugs in the shelter.

4. When Naomi saw the enormous amount of grain Ruth had collected on her first day in the field and that it was on the property of a man named Boaz, her whole attitude toward life changed for the better.

5. Naomi announced that that very same Boaz was a close relative of her deceased husband—indeed a "kinsman-redeemer."

Questions for Thought and Reflection

1. Was the task of a kinsman-redeemer's marriage limited to a deceased brother who had not yet produced any children? Was Elimelekh a "brother" to Boaz? Did that affect the task Boaz was obligated to fill?

2. What role does the Hebrew term *hesed* play in this story? How does that term fit into the covenants God made with Israel?

3. Why would God choose a pagan foreigner such as Ruth to be in the line of producing the ancestor of David and thus have a part in the Messianic genealogy?

4. Where do you see the doctrine of providence operating in this chapter rather than happenings being attributed to just chance?

5. What role does Boaz's foreman play in this chapter? Does he report anything negative about Ruth?

Lesson 4

Naomi the Matchmaker Proposes a Threshing-floor Encounter with Boaz

Ruth 3:1–18

In the well-known musical *Fiddler on the Roof,* Tevye's daughter, Tzeitel, sings a very catchy song: "Matchmaker, matchmaker, make me a match, find me a find, catch me a catch … Make me a perfect match." Was this song to Yenta modeled after Naomi's plans for Ruth? It might seem so; Boaz appears to be the same age as Naomi, yet she consistently addresses Ruth as "my daughter" in vv. 2:8; 3:10, 11, just as Yenta's best shot at finding a husband for Tzeitel turned out to be a marriage to a gentleman who was old enough to be her father. However, in Ruth's case, Boaz turned out to be outstanding in character and achievements, even though he too was older. Boaz and Ruth were well-matched, so Naomi did an excellent job as a matchmaker! Let us examine how she did it.

Naomi the Matchmaker's Instructions to Ruth – 3:1–7

Naomi feels responsible for locating a home for her daughter-in-law Ruth—a home where she would be well provided for (v. 3:1). Having come to that conclusion, that reasoning left Naomi only one choice: What about Boaz? Is he not one of our kinsman-redeemers?

Sadly, some evangelical interpreters tend to read more into this narrative than the bare-bones narrative supports. For example, one recent commentator told the story this way after noting that Hosea 9:1 "links threshing floors with illicit sex":

> Naomi proposes her risky proposition to Ruth [in which] …
> Naomi sends Ruth there at night to enchant the man Boaz. Night

is considered to be time for sinful not for righteous deeds. …
What does Naomi hope will happen?

The best response to such innuendos comes from Cyril Barber: "In the
case of Ruth and Boaz … any hint of moral impropriety is unfounded."[1]
Ruth carried out Naomi's plan in a discreet and godly manner. In fact,
Boaz showed real concern for any misinterpretation that might come from
Ruth's actions, so he urged her to leave the threshing-floor as early as
possible, before the full morning light.

To be sure, a woman like Ruth could hardly walk right up to Boaz in
the middle of the field and say, "Will you marry me?" Added to this crazy
idea is the fact that a mere seven weeks had elapsed since the two had met
at the beginning of the barley harvest, so there was little time for any
progress to be made. But Naomi had an idea that took an altogether novel
path. She instructed Ruth as follows:

> Is not Boaz … a kinsman of ours. Tonight, he will be winnowing
> barley on the threshing floor. Wash and perfume yourself and put
> on your best clothes. Then go down to the threshing floor, but
> don't let him know you are there until he has finished eating and
> drinking. When he lies down, note the place where he is lying.
> Then go and uncover his feet and lie down. He will tell you what
> to do. (3:2–4)

The threshing floor was a circular level area that usually measured 25 to
40 feet in diameter. It was often a site near the grain field, preferably on an
elevated spot exposed to the wind, to winnow the lighter husk on the grain
when the grains were thrown up into the air so the wind could catch that
light covering on the grain. The threshing-floor site was prepared by
removing all the stones from the circle; the stones often became the border
to retain the grain. Then the dirt was wet down and tamped into as hard a
surface as possible, which acted as the flat surface or a type of table for the

---

[1]. Cyril J. Barber, *Ruth: A Story of God's Grace*, 88.

heavier fallen grains. Since there were no secure means of protecting one's grain, it required the landowner to sleep by his pile until he had finished winnowing it and arranged for its disposal, sale or storage.

After Boaz had finished eating and drinking, he "was in good spirits," so, "he went over to lie down at the far end of the grain pile" (v. 3:7). It was now time for Ruth to make her move, so she "approached quietly, uncovered his feet and lay down" (v. 7b). One can almost feel the silence of the surrounding fields as the hour quietly slips by midnight. Still nothing is happening as the scene closes and the stars keep watch over the grain pile with the landowner sleeping soundly after a day of heavy work. Meanwhile, a young maiden curiously lies at his feet in the improvised bed.

Boaz's Sudden and Startling Awakening – 3:8–13

"In the middle of the night something startled the man, and he turned and discovered a woman lying at his feet" (v. 8). The word translated "startled" is from the Hebrew *harad*, denoting "great fear" or "trembling." His first instinct was to "turn," from the rare Hebrew *lapat*, meaning something like "to grasp" or "to turn oneself." Boaz must have twisted himself around to see who or what was at his feet, covering itself with part of his bed cover or his garment.

"Who are you?" Boaz demanded. The woman at his feet quickly answered, perhaps in a coquettish tone, "I am your servant, Ruth!" (v. 9). "Spread the corner of your garment over me since you are a kinsman-redeemer," she continued (v. 9b).

The act of spreading one's garment or blanket over another was tantamount to a pledge to follow through with a plan to marry that person. This act would serve symbolically much like the giving of an engagement ring in many cultures of our day. This euphemistic idiom is used as a pledge for marriage in Ezekiel 16:8 and Malachi 2:16. Even today, this same custom still exists among Arabs and in parts of the marriage culture in India. In Ruth's case, this act signified that she was requesting to be moved from the status of an unprotected widow to the protective care of a husband—Boaz, for instance!

Of even greater interest is Ruth's use of "garment" in v. 3:9. The word *kanap*, meaning "wing" or "corner of a garment," is the same word she used in v. 2:12. It refers to both a bird's protecting wings and a skirt or garment that covered or protected the wearer. Previously she had used this image to speak of coming under the "wing" of God's protective care, but now she was offering to place herself under Boaz's "wings."

Boaz, now fully awake, realized what was going on, so he replied to her request for marriage thus:

> The LORD bless you, my daughter. This kindness is greater than that which you showed earlier: You have not run after younger men, whether rich or poor. And now, my daughter, don't be afraid. I will do for you all you ask. All my fellow townsmen know you are a woman of noble character. Although it is true that I am near of kin, there is a kinsmen-redeemer nearer than I. Stay here for the night, and in the morning if he wants to redeem, good; but if he is not willing, as surely as the LORD lives, I will do it. Lie here until morning. (3:10–13)

It is clear from his word of blessing that Boaz was not offended by Ruth's actions and request for marriage. He may have been impressed by her boldness, for at that time it was countercultural for a woman to propose marriage to a man, or a younger person to propose to an older one, or even a field worker to a landowner. In his view, Ruth's "last kindness" (i.e., her proposal to him of a Levirate marriage) was "better than the first" (i.e., her earlier kindnesses towards Naomi, v. 10). Moreover, Boaz called Ruth a "woman of noble character" (*'aishet hayil*). He was ascribing to her the lovely words inscribed in Proverbs 31:10–31, a woman whose "works praise her in the gates." Boaz completed his speech by noting that all the people of that area knew that Ruth was a real "woman of worth" (v. 11).

How did Ruth achieve such a high reputation among the Bethlehemites, when just less than two months before she had arrived as an unknown foreigner? She was far too humble to have sounded her own trumpet. Instead, she had served in the fields as Naomi's servant and worked without complaint in the heat of the harvest time to help her mother-in-law survive. But that is the key, for such humble commitment to duty must not have escaped the wide knowledge of the community. She was especially highly regarded because of her loving kindness to her mother-in-law.

As both Boaz and Ruth were characterized as persons of honor, it is important to note that there is nothing illicit in this story or any evidence of a sexual encounter between them. Some interpreters of this text try to suggest that "uncover his feet" (v. 3:4) is a euphemism for nudity (see Lev. 18:6–19; 20:11, 17–21; Ezek. 22:10, NASB). But in context, and since Boaz and Ruth are honorable, this interpretation is inappropriate. Moreover, the Hebrew word here for "feet" is purposely different in those other contexts.

Boaz Loads Ruth's Apron with Barley – 3:14–18

It may well be that because of Boaz's assurance that this matter would be settled that very next morning in the city gates (where all such legal matters took place before ten elders of the town), after he had given a much closer kinsman-redeemed the first opportunity to marry Ruth, that because of this assurance, she must have fallen off into a dreamy sleep for the reminder of that night, resting in the glow that Boaz cared deeply about her welfare and future.

In the intervening time, Naomi apparently was not aware that her plan had a serious flaw, for she must have forgotten or did not realize there was another kinsman-redeemer who outranked Boaz with prior claims. But that raises another question: How in such a small town as Bethlehem could Naomi not have known about this other contender for the position of kinsman-redeemer? We cannot answer that question, but it was enough that God in his providence knew all about this situation, so we do not worry about this matter!

Boaz cautioned Ruth to stay where she had taken up her place until the morning light began to appear (v. 3:14). However, Ruth should leave before anyone could recognize her, for Boaz did not want any gossip going around that a woman had visited his threshing floor that night and might start to imagine scenarios that were not true (v. 3:14b).

Then Boaz asked Ruth to bring her apron she wore and to hold it out. When she did, Boaz filled with it with six measures of barley, which possibly weighed about eighty pounds of grain Boaz gave to Ruth and her mother-in-law (vv. 15, 17). Boaz had to help Ruth mount that load on her back as she set out for home. Boaz's goal was that Ruth should not go back to her mother-in-law empty (v. 17).

When Ruth arrived in Bethlehem, Naomi, who was always filled with good counsel, urged Ruth to "wait … until you find out what happens, for the man will not rest until the matter is settled today" (v. 18). God is at work, so it is important now for Ruth and Naomi to just "sit tight" and watch and see what the Lord of the universe will do!

Conclusions

1. Naomi continued to be concerned for Ruth. She wanted to find a home for her so that she would be well provided for.

2. Since Boaz was a close relative who could perform the duties of a kinsman-redeemer, Ruth, even though she was a younger woman, must put the question to him in a private setting when all the others had left for the day.

3. Naomi gave Ruth some cosmetic instructions on how she might make herself more attractive to Boaz than what he had seen her appear as she worked in the fields.

4. Boaz was suddenly awakened in the middle of the night as his feet felt something very abnormal. He found out it was Ruth whom he labeled "a woman of worth" and "noble character."

5. Boaz sent Ruth home early the next morning loaded down perhaps with as much as 80 pounds of barley grains.

Questions for Thought and Reflection

1. How should a person act when they find that their lives have suddenly, and apparently prematurely, culminated in a dead end with the death of a partner or a similar life-halting tragedy?

2. Why is it that we are told so frequently to simply wait to see what God is going to do when we would rather be active making things happen?

3. What sorts of actions do we see in Ruth that qualify her as a "woman of valor," one of "noble character." Is the woman described in Proverbs 31:10–31 even a real possibility for women today, or is the picture painted just idealistic?

4. How important is it to dress up and to use perfume in order to attract a mate for life?

5. What risks were Ruth and Naomi taking in going to Boaz's threshing floor at night?

Lesson 5

Failed Negotiations with Ploni 'Almoni
Ruth 4:1–22

Boaz left the threshing-floor and headed off to the town gate where all official business was conducted and where he was able to meet with the kinsman-redeemer, who had a prior claim in his relationship to Elimelekh. He had the "right of first refusal" and was first in line to redeem the property of his deceased relative, Elimelekh (4:1). In those days, all town business was conducted at the city or town gate (Gen. 34:20; 1 Kgs. 22:10; Amos 5:10, 12, 15; Prov. 22:22; 31:23), so that is where Boaz went to settle this situation.

Boaz's Registry of the Real Estate Sale at the Town Gate –4:1b-8

Once there, Boaz took his seat where he waited for this kinsman redeemer to be "passing by." When Boaz saw him, he called out to him, "Come over here, my friend [ploni 'almoni] and sit down" (v. 4:1b). The expression *ploni 'almoni* is a type of wordplay where meaningless rhyming words are brought together to form a new idiom, such as "hodgepodge," "helter-skelter" or "heebie-jeebies." In this case the words could be rendered something akin to "What's-his-name," "Whatchamacallit," "Mr. So-and-So," or even "Hey, you there!"

This relative is never named in this narrative, either because it slipped Boaz's memory or because he refused to perform the rite of kinsman redeemer which was so disgraceful that it was best to just forget his name. So, this "Mr. Nobody" came over and sat down with the ten elders of Bethlehem in time to hear Boaz suddenly talking about a sale of a property that belonged to a relative named Elimelekh.

Previously, there had been no mention of the sale of Elimelekh's land, but it was now also for sale. As Naomi had no sons left, the opportunity arose for a relative to redeem that land and add it to their estates. Boaz put the prospect of the sale of the land up to Mr. What's-His-Name in this manner:

> "Naomi, who has come back from Moab, is selling the piece of land that belonged to our brother Elimelekh. I thought I should bring the matter to your attention and suggest that you buy it in the presence of these seated here and in the presence of the elders of my people. If you will redeem it, do so. But if you will not, tell me, so I will know. For no one has the right to do it except you, and I am next in line. (4:2–4)

Mr. So-and-So, however, was quick to agree to take up this excellent offer, for he outrightly affirmed: "I will redeem it" (v. 4:4d). But just then, Boaz sprung some additional information he had been holding back: "On the day you buy the land from Naomi and from Ruth the Moabitess, you acquire the dead man's widow to maintain the name of the dead with his property." (v. 4:5)

That changed everything for the relative, who protested: "Then I cannot redeem it because I might endanger my own estate. You redeem it yourself. I cannot do it" (v. 6). In effect he said, "I'm out; go ahead and redeem it yourself!" Since there was a young widow involved, he could see that he would barely get possession of the land when suddenly, this widow might have a son born to her and the land would then be his and not the possession of him who redeemed it.

This real estate transaction called for "the ceremony of the shoe." As the written record of this event was likely written years after, it was necessary to explain this obsolete custom to a new generation of readers of Ruth. Deuteronomy 25:9 gives an idea of what it involved. This Mr. Nobody was called on at to take off his sandal and give it to Boaz in the presence of witnesses at the city gate to show he was turning down his responsibility to redeem this "offer." The widow Naomi was not present, as she did not follow through with the rest of the ceremony, which had a provision for her to "spit" in the face of the one who rejected his role as kinsman-redeemer. That would show what was expected of a real relative!

"Acquire it yourself," the relative told Boaz as he removed his sandal and gave it to him. This was the legitimate method of legalizing the transaction in Israel at that time! The scandal of a relative turning down his role of redeeming a widow in such a situation was so serious that it called for a public scolding that would make other Israelites think twice before they too turned down such an obligation (v. 4:7).

Boaz Declares His Intention to Marry Ruth, Widow of Mahlon – 4:9-12

The negotiations with the dissenting kinsman-redeemer now over, Boaz addressed the elders and the witnesses at the town gate. He announced his intention to marry Ruth and to raise up a family for Elimelekh and Ruth's deceased son, her former husband Mahlon (v. 4:9). It would be recorded that Boaz had bought from Naomi all the property Elimelekh had owned, as well as that he had acquired Ruth the Moabitess, widow of Mahlon, to be his wife. He would do so to maintain the name of the dead along with his property so that the name of Elimelekh would not disappear from the memory of his family or from the town records. Boaz called on those in the gate area to affirm that they indeed were witnesses to these facts (v. 10).

The elders and all those in the gate area, which constituted something like the settings for our town-hall meetings, heard all of them say, "We are witnesses!" (v. 11). This same group of people added:

"May the LORD make the woman who is coming into your house like Rachel and Leah, who together built up the house of Israel. May you have standing in Ephrathah and be famous in Bethlehem, through the offspring the LORD gives you by this young woman, may your family be like that of Perez, whom Tamar bore to Judah." (4:11–12)

The references to Rachel and Leah (note the inverse order of their marriages here) are of course allusions to the two daughters of Laban, the Aramean/Syrian, for whom Jacob worked seven years each. Leah was the more fruitful wife, who regularly gave Jacob sons, long before Rachel finally conceived Joseph and bore Benjamin to him.

What was being said in this prayer for blessing on the newly married couple was a prayer for Ruth to experience the intervention of God so that she would be as fertile as both of these women. The expression "to build up a house" is a familiar one for establishing a family by means of having a progeny and a seed as Psalm 127:1 reminds us: "Unless the LORD builds the house, its builders labor in vain."

But there was a second blessing, directed to Boaz: "May you have standing in Ephrathah and be famous in Bethlehem" (v. 4:11c). Once again, the same word, *'ashet hayil,* is used here as is found in Proverbs 31:10, but this time it is rendered not as "woman of worth/value" but as "a man of standing"—*'aish hayil,* or a "man of valor"; cf. Ruth 2:1, 3:11). *Hayil* can be translated as someone of "wealth," "virtue," "valor," "worth," or "standing."

Thus, the prayer of those who had gathered in the gate area was that Boaz would be a man of great character, worth and reputation in the community of Israel. This prayer was cast in the typical Hebrew poetical form of "synonymous parallelism," where the first line is further explained by the second, so both are seen to mean essentially the same thing. Accordingly, the two names of "Ephrathah" and "Bethlehem" point to the same place, but they use the older and newer names for the place. The two terms "being famous" and "having worth/standing" again are used to mean the same thing in this prayer of blessing.

The third benediction in v. 12 is that the "offspring coming from the LORD coming through this young woman named Ruth, will be like Perez, whom Tamar bore to Judah." This references the story in Genesis 38, where Tamar, after she had lost husband number one named Er, Judah's oldest son, then also lost as a husband Er's brother Onan. She did not get to marry the third brother, as expected according to the Levitate law, a brother named Shelah. Judah feared this woman was somehow jinxed, so he did not let his son Shelah marry her. But Tamar conceived a plan to trick Judah by disguising herself as a local prostitute and getting him to have sex with her. Thus, she became pregnant from this tryst, and she conceived the twins Perez and Zerah by Judah, her father-in-law. Here Perez is mentioned because he was the ancestor of the clan of Boaz in Bethlehem. Genesis 38, then, is a story of a possible levirate marriage, just as the book of Ruth is. The community, therefore, prayed that there would be a great increase to the family of Boaz, just as there was in the family of Judah, which became one of the largest and most outstanding tribes in Israel.

This prayer, with its references to Tamar and Perez, might be a warning for all those in Bethlehem, especially those women who might be inclined to gossip about a foreigner, indeed a Moabitess, coming into this family line in Bethlehem, to take another look into their own closets, for their ancestral line had some ghosts in it as well. Instead, they should look how gracious God had been, first, not only forgiving these ancestors of their transgressions, but second, looking at how gracious the Lord had been in giving to them such prominent places and such a providential number of instances of his work among them as a nation.

Ruth Conceives a Son Named Obed – 4:13–17

This section gives an excellent picture of how the Lord works with mortals who trust him, for Ruth, when she was Mahlon's wife, was unable to conceive. Now, though, as the wife of Boaz, when she obviously was older, and Boaz likewise must have been as old and a part of Naomi's generation, was able to conceive (v. 13). So, Ruth fell into the class of women who gave birth under most unusual circumstances, such as Hannah's birth of Samuel and Elizabeth's birth of John the Immerser. No wonder the women who heard about Ruth's wonderful gift of a son, praised God, and cheered up Naomi, saying:

"Praise be to the LORD, who this day has not left you without a kinsman-redeemer. May he become famous throughout Israel. He will renew your life and sustain you in your old age. For your daughter-in-law who loves you and who is better to you than seven sons, has given him birth." (4:14–15)

Naomi was thrilled with the appearance of this child, for she took him and laid him on her lap and cared for him and nursed him. The women who lived in Bethlehem credited to Ruth's mother-in-law the newborn son as if Naomi had conceived him, and they named him Obed, meaning "servant," perhaps an abbreviation for Obadiah, "servant of the LORD" (v. 4:17). Obed, however, became the father of Jesse, who became the father of David.

The Generational Line of Perez Down to David of Bethlehem – 4:18–22

Some wonder why the last five verses begin the line of Perez (v. 4:18). The name Perez was introduced into this narrative by the mention of Tamar's name, but others say that ten names here at the end of this story were needed to balance the ten names with which this text began in 1:1–5, in which Ruth completes the first list and David completes the last list. In this final genealogical list, the name of Boaz occurs as seventh from Perez. This genealogical list extends from the days of the patriarchs until the days of the judges. As usual, some names are skipped, for the list of names spans eight or nine centuries. The first five names lead up to the exodus, and the last five follow it.

Boaz's father was Salmon, which would mean Rahab, the non-Israelite barmaid, who was saved in the destruction of Jericho for hiding and saving Joshua's spies (Josh. 2:6; Mt. 1:5), appears to be Ruth's other mother-in-law. Rahab also was a foreigner who forsook her people and put her trust in the Lord, thereby saving her own family, as Israel conquered the Land.

Conclusions

1. Boaz knew there was an unnamed relative who had greater and prior claims to redeeming Ruth, if he chose to pursue those claims. Why was Naomi unaware of this situation?

2. This *ploni 'almoni* was willing to buy the land owned by Elimelekh, which would increase his estate, but when he learned he had to marry Ruth as part of the deal, he backed out of it.

3. Mr. So-and-So had to surrender one of his sandals as proof that he was relinquishing his responsibilities of redeeming Ruth and the property of his relative.

4. The townspeople who were the witnesses at the gate-hearing blessed Ruth for becoming Boaz's wife, as they prayed, she might be as fertile as Leah and Rachel were to Jacob.

5. The child born to Ruth was Obed, who would be in the famous line leading to King David of Bethlehem.

Questions for Thought and Reflection

1. Why do you think God made Ruth fertile being Boaz's wife after she had been without children for ten years as Mahlon's wife?

2. Why does the genealogy at the end of the book of Ruth begin with the name of Perez? Why are only ten names chosen to cover some 800 to 900 years of time?

3. Why does the Hebrew word *shuv* (return) occur some 15 times in Ruth with three occurring in 1:6–22? Does Obed being called the "Restorer" of life possibly have anything to do with this word?

4. What items in this narrative are "restored" or "returned" once again?

5. How do Boaz's actions vindicate the fact that he was a man of great character and standing in the community?

ESTHER

A Girl with Both
Inner and Outer Beauty

Lesson 1

Introduction to the Book of Esther

No Direct References to God

Esther has the distinction of being the only book in the Bible that does not make a direct reference to God. Nowhere is he mentioned in the ten chapters, so the question is, where is God hiding in this book? And where can we find his righteous people? There is a noticeable absence of any prayers, sacrifices, or praise for the living God. Neither of the two main characters, Esther, and Mordecai, give any evidence of being spiritual or praying persons (unless we accept six additions that some Greek versions add to the text—more on that later).

In fact, Mordecai, Esther's uncle, who had adopted her, even encouraged her to hide her identify (vv. 2:10, 20) rather than reveal her Jewishness, which of course would have revealed her relationship to the Lord.

So, what is it about the book of Esther that should help us in our walk with the God above all other gods and Lord above all other lords? How did this book make it into the canon of Scripture? What is the message we are supposed to derive from this book? To begin to answer these questions, let us investigate the book's historical background.

The Historical Background of Esther

As related from the first verse of the book of Esther, the events in this book took place during the reign of the Persian King Xerxes, also called Ahasuerus, who ruled from 486–465 B.C.E. Those dates would place the events in this book between the completion of the second Temple in

Jerusalem under Governor Zerubbabel during the reign of another Persian, Darius I (516 B.C.E.) and Ezra's arrival with a small part of the exiled remnant from Babylon and Persia, who moved to Jerusalem in 458 B.C.E. under Artaxerxes I. Many of the Jewish people, however, preferred to remain in exile and to live in the eastern part of the Persian Empire. As shown in the discovery of the archaeological Murashu texts from *Nippur*, some of the Jews were indeed prospering well in Persia despite being exiled from Judah.

That background does not tell us much about how to view the book's meaning, so let us look at its structure.

The Structure of the Book

With the absence of God's name, any reference to prayer, etc., the book of Esther presents a troubling presence to the canon of the Old Testament. Yet despite its lack of a theological emphasis, it has an important connection with the Jewish people. In fact, T. K. Beal noticed the Babylonian Talmud found a connection between Esther and the Torah. In Hebrew, consonantal text may be written "pointed" or "un-pointed," i.e., with or without vowel marks. In Deuteronomy 31:18, notes Beal, the first-person imperfect verb 'str ("I will hide") is identical to the un-pointed Hebrew consonants used for Esther's name, meaning "I will hide [my face from this rebellious people]."[1] From a rabbinic point of view, this allows Esther to be linked to Moses' Book of the Law, even when there is not direct quote or allusion to the Torah. This is a stretch, but it is possible!

More to the point, most have noted that Esther begins and ends with a pair of feasts that mirror each other (Est. 1:3,5; 9:18–19), both given by the king. In the middle of the book, however, just where the climax of the plot comes, Esther herself gives two feasts—one for the king and one for Haman (5:4–8; 7:1). The Hebrew term for a "feast," *mishteh*, occurs 20

---

1. T. K. Beal, *The Book in Hiding: Gender, Ethnicity, Annihilation and Esther*, 116–17.

times in this book but only 28 times in the rest of the Old Testament. Moreover, one of the key purposes of this book is to explain how the Feast of Purim came into the life and experience of Israel. So thus far, we can say Esther is indeed a book of "feasts."

Karen Jobes,[2] for instance, picks up the repetition of these feasts as a primary motif. But she instead points to the three pairs of feasts at the beginning, climax and conclusion of Esther, which were also marked by a sudden turn of events. Aristotle[3] referred to them using the Greek peripetery, a literary term used to designate a story that contains a sudden reversal or turn of events from where one expected the story to go or what seemed to be its intended end. So, what is so significant about such a turn of events to the understanding of this book?

Well, interestingly, these "reversals" tend to pivot on what at first seems an insignificant incident of the king having a sleepless night in which he called for the reading to him of the official record of past events (Est. 6:1). In this way, the peripety of an incidental event shifted the focus away from what humans were doing and therefore led the reader to look for another controlling force, one beyond the human level, that could reverse what first was the outcome. That One, of course, was none other than the God of the universe! Perhaps this is where God has been hiding!

But the plot thickens; Haman is specifically referred to as an "Agagite" (3:1). This gives the contest even more tension, for the identity of Haman as an Agagite gives us another clue that this story has its roots far back in history. Agag was the king of the Amalekites at the same time Saul became the first king of Israel (1 Sam. 15). The Amalekites, who had made war on Israel during their wilderness wanderings when they left Egypt, focused their attacks on those who were lagging behind, weary and worn out (Deut. 25:17–19).

---

2. Karen H. Jobes, *Esther (NIV Application Commentary)*, 154–58.

3. Aristotle, *Rhetorica* 1.11.24.

As a result of this inhumane act, God gave the charge to "blot out the memory" of the Amalekites, for their reprehensible attacks drew his wrath. But Saul disobeyed God and spared King Agag's life, along with many animals he planned to offer in a huge sacrifice to God (1 Sam. 15:1–3). Because of this disobedience (and other forms of it), God rejected Saul as king over Israel, chiding him that "to obey was better than sacrifice and to hearken was better than the fat of rams."

There is more to the story: Saul was a Benjamite whose father was Kish (1 Sam. 9:21, 14:51). Mordecai is likewise said to be a Benjamite, who also is said to be the "son" of a man also named Kish (v. 2:5). In this role, Mordecai appears to act in this narrative as a new Saul. The relative clause in the Hebrew text refers not to Mordecai himself as the antecedent but to his grandfather Kish, who was taken into exile along with King Jeconiah, also called King Jehoiachin. Mordecai, then, would be a "son" in the usual Hebrew sense of a "descendant" or a later "relative" of Kish. Mentioning Kish, however, strengthens the parallel connection between Mordecai and Haman, just as there was one between Saul and Agag.

Thus, Esther's story continues an ancient hostility rooted in the contest between Israel and the Amalekites that had long tentacles in the histories of both nations. However, now Israel seems more vulnerable than ever, for now that Israel is exiled in Persia, she has no king, no army, no prophet, no land, no temple, no sacrifices, no priesthood to resort to–she is more exposed than ever. Unless there is a dramatic "reversal" of affairs (i.e., unless God dramatically intervenes), she will be hopelessly and unmercifully slaughtered.

There is one more shocking surprise, for Haman the Agagite cast the dice (*pur*) to determine on which day the Jews of Persia would be destroyed. In this case, it was not a game of chance but a pagan divination to determine the day Haman's gods would give him victory over the Jewish people, whom he wanted to obliterate from the kingdom. Here is the surprise: Haman rolled the dice in the first month of the Jewish year, in the month of Nisan—and it came out as being on the thirteenth day of

Nisan (v. 3:12). This edict, which would have proclaimed the death of all Jews, went out, ironically enough, on the eve of Passover, which took place on the next day, i.e., the fourteenth. Thus, Haman rolled the dice on the night commemorating Israel's deliverance from death in Egypt as the death angel killed all the firstborn of Egypt but "passed over" the houses of the Israelites.

Thus, on a similar night, many centuries later in Shushan, Persia, another declaration of death went out, only this time it was against the people of Israel at the hands of Haman the Agagite. How about that for another surprise! Was this pure chance, or was the God of providence watching over his people to teach them something? This must be a significant move on a significant date! God's promise to the patriarchs and to Moses and David made it clear that the rolling of the dice (by Haman or anyone else) would not determine the destiny of God's people: He alone would determine what Israel would be and what would happen to them! Anyway, God had already promised how things would turn out for Israel, so how could a set of dice make it different?

Therefore, Esther in Persia, like Joseph in Egypt and Daniel in Babylon, was placed strategically in a foreign Gentile court at the top worldly power of that day, and she was there at the precise moment that God wanted her to be there so she could be used to deliver his people.

The Feast of Purim

The word *puru* ("die, lot") is a Persian word that appears in the Scriptures only in Esther. The Hebrew equivalent is *goral*, "stone" (vv. 3:7, 9:24). Archaeologists have found dice with *puru* written on them. Since this word was unknown to the Israelites, how did this feast and its name come together if they had no historical connections, as some try to say? Moreover, originally this feast was known at first as the "day of Mordecai" (2 Macc. 15:36). But more than that is not known to us. However, the fact that the names "Feast of Purim" and the "Day of Mordecai" have both come down to us gives us confidence that the book of Esther has a historical basis.

The Providence of God

Though this book does not mention God's name in any explicit way, it is difficult to deny there is a strong theology of the providence of God behind and within this book. All the Scriptures speak of the constant care God has given to the nation Israel; all that happened to her was from his hand. Hebrew does not have a synonym for the English word "Providence," but God's ruling and over-ruling hand can clearly be seen. And not only was God interested in the affairs of the nation, he was also interested in the lives of individuals as well. Proverbs 20:24 says, "A person's steps are directed by the Lord." Psalm 73:23: "I am always with you; you hold me by my right hand."

The Jewish people thought their ways and plights were hidden from the Lord, but they had not been disregarded by their God, for he had gone ahead of them and prepared his instruments of deliverance as he placed Esther in the courts of Persia and gave favor to Mordecai and ultimately raised both of them to positions of power.

That God overruled evil so that good might come to his people does not mean that all the methods used by Mordecai and Esther were approved by God! For example, we do not know what Esther was required to do when she took her turn going in to be judged by the king. In v. 2:14, she went in to be with the king in the evening and returned in the morning, no longer to be left with the Persian official in charge of the virgins but now with the man in charge of the concubines.

This implies the king was guilty of adultery and Esther was guilty of marrying someone who was not a believer. The Bible does not comment on this. But the mere mention of a situation does not mean God nor the Bible approved of all that went on. He was still able to bring his purposes out of it despite the presence of any sin committed by these mortals. The truth of the matter is as Mordecai instructed Esther: "If you remain silent at this time, relief and deliverance for the Jews will arise from another place" (v. 4:14). God was not handicapped by this one method of delivering his people.

Six Additions to the Book of Esther

Six chapter-length additions, totaling 105 verses, have been added to some versions of the book of Esther. They are usually designated by the capital letters A–F, and they survive only in two Greek versions: the Septuagint and the Alpha text. The important note about these additions is that they supply the missing religious language Esther is missing, especially A, C, D, F. Additions B and E are official memos from the Persian king. All the additions fit very cleanly and comfortably into the narrative of the Hebrew text. Scholars judge that B and E originated in Greek, but the other four have had arguments in favor of both a Hebrew and a Greek origin.

Jerome, when he made his Vulgate Latin translation of the Bible in the fourth century, did not include these six passages in their context because they were not in Hebrew. He put them together as an appendix to Esther. It was claimed that an Egyptian Jew added these texts to the body of the text sometime around 100 B.C.E. Here the additions as Jerome placed them in his appendix:

Addition A: Mordecai's dream –11:2–12:6

Addition B: Edict of Artaxerxes against the Jews – 13:1–7

Addition C: Prayers of Mordecai and Esther – 13:8–14:19

Addition D: Esther's Appearance Before the King – 15:1–16

Addition E: Decree of Artaxerxes on behalf of the Jews – 16:1–24

Addition F: Interpretation of Mordecai's Dream – 10:4–11:1

Conclusion: The Danger of Antisemitism

Throughout the history of the world, there has been a serious reaction against and opposition to the Jewish people; the opposition of the Persian court was not a historical nuance. As far back as the times of the Egyptian Pharaoh of the exodus, there was an attempt to try to destroy the Jewish people. This hostility has been repeated by many dictators, such as Hitler. But there is more going on here than an outright antipathy for a particular people; it is actually a manifestation of Satan's work in this world. His enmity against the Jews is his attempt to defeat none other than God himself and his redemptive plan for the world (John 15:18–20).

> "If the world hates you, keep in mind that it hated me first. If you belonged to the world, it would love you as its own. As it is, you do not belong to the world, but I have chosen you out of the world. That is why the world hates you. Remember what I told you: 'A servant is not greater than his master.' If they persecuted me, they will persecute you also. If they obeyed my teaching, they will obey yours also."

So, Believers must be careful in this regard. We are commanded to love everyone, especially Jews, for regardless of race or anything else, we are to be alert to the enemy's tactics in which he tries to get us to hate others. In this sense, then, Haman is a paradigm and a model of such God-haters, by which all subsequent enemies of the Jews and believers will be judged. Remember Genesis 12:3 on the consequences of cursing Jewish people! Recall that at first those who followed the Messiah, Yeshua, were Jewish believers in overwhelmingly large numbers. Paul always began his ministry first in the synagogues and only went to the Gentiles after rejection started to arise against his preaching. So, the split between the Jewish and Gentile believers, who followed what at first was just called "the Way," seems to have begun already around the mid-2nd century C.E., when a Church Father named Justin Martyr (c. 100–165) wrote *Dialogue with Trypho*. In it, he debates a Jewish scholar named Trypho, who in chapter 11 made the point that would ultimately become "replacement theology" (a view that claims the promises made to Abraham, Isaac, Jacob and David were later given to the Church in Christian times, because Israel had failed to obey God's word). In chapter 11 Justin wrongly concluded:

> We (Christians) have been led to God through the crucified Christ, and we are [now] the true spiritual Israel, and the descendants of Judah, Jacob, Isaac and Abraham who, though uncircumcised, was approved and blessed by God because of his faith and was called the father of many nations.

In dialogue 119, Justin went on to wrongly claim:

> We Christians shall inherit the Holy Land ... but it is not you (Jews to whom it was first given) in whom there is no faith.

Justin argued that Israel had been totally deposed of her promises she originally had in the Abrahamic and Davidic Covenants; thus, what had been promised to Israel, including the land of Israel, now belonged to the Church. This is the beginning of "supersessionism" (the Church "sits in the seat" Israel once held by God's promise), the start of "replacement theology" in Christianity.

Emperor Constantine gathered the bishops together in the thirtieth year of his reign, as well as at the Council of Nicaea (325 C.E.). There, he declared the celebration of Christian Easter should no longer be linked with the celebration of the Jewish Passover, as it had been practiced up to that time. Said the Emperor, "It is unbecoming that on the holiest of festivals, we should follow the customs of the Jews; henceforth let us have nothing in common with this odious people." The break with the Jewish side of the believing community became even more apparent.

In 387, a man who was converted to Christ late in his life, Augustine, was baptized outside of Rome. He too would adopt replacement theology after earlier seeing God's promises to Abraham and the Jewish people as enduring, as God himself is eternal in his person and his word. Because of his later stature in the Church and his prolific writings, he has had a huge impact on the theology of the Roman Catholic Church, Protestant Reformed Theology, and much of the rest of the Christian Church with his replacement theology.

Even more damaging to Jewish-Christian relations were the series of sermons given by the famously gifted preacher and Bishop of Antioch, John Chrysostom, in 387 C.E. Justin Martyr and Augustine were milder in their deviation from the teaching of Scripture, but Chrysostom's rhetoric in eight of his sermons knew no controls or bounds. He stressed that the Jewish people had "killed God" and that was why the promises made to them had to be given over to others.

However, the teaching of the book of Esther must be related to the teaching of Romans 9–11. There, God declares he is not finished with the Jewish people, but will fulfill his promise made to Abraham, Isaac, Jacob and David. God will not go back on his promise of sending his Son through the line of Abraham and David. Nor will he revise his promise about giving the Land to Israel. The promises of God are forever true and irrevocable!

Scripture demonstrates that God's purpose is to preserve the Jewish people and nation from extinction, whether that attempt will come from the hands of the Egyptians, Assyrians, Babylonians, Persians, Nazis, or Arab nations. Put in its broadest terms, this preservation was because the nation was being prepared for the honor of receiving the Son of God on their soil, not once but a second time as history concludes.

Queen Esther in her day fulfilled her part in saving the nation from destruction. Later, Yeshua came to this place where east meets west, where the continents of Africa, Europe and Asia meet, to gather together all things in himself. Therefore, as hard as it is for Arabs and Jewish people to accept this truth from Scripture, God himself will complete the promise he made to Abraham, Isaac, Jacob, David and in the New Covenant as well: He will send Messiah back to descend on the Mount of Olives once more. Before that happens, he will give the Land back to the Jewish people, and then he will come dwell in the midst of his people to rule and reign on earth and in this Jewish people, all the families of the earth will be blessed (Gen. 12:2–3; 2 Sam. 7:16–19; Jer. 31:31–34).

Lesson 2

The Winner of the
Miss Persia Beauty Contest Is…

Esther 2:1–23

After making a momentous decision, people do not always immediately realize the implications of all they have just brought about! This was certainly true of the decision King Xerxes had just decreed about his queen, Vashti! His noble counselor Memucan had suggested to the king that he issue a royal decree, not only that Vashti never again enter his presence but that her position be given to someone "better" than she (v. 1:19). By "better," the implication was that she should be replaced by someone more compliant with the king's orders—one who would obey her husband. Yet this search for a "replacement wife" made no statement about a "character assessment" or promise to faithfully obey her lord the king.

This search for a beauty queen did not involve some form of competition to gain entrance to the contest; instead, all young virgins already were in the competition by virtue of their living in the empire. No permission was needed to draft a woman for this contest, just as no permission from the parents was needed to draft young sons as palace eunuchs. It made no difference if parents had other plans for these sons or daughters; the empire could choose who they wanted, and that was that! Nor could girls say, as some do today, "My body, my choice!" In the Medo-Persian world, all that a person possessed, including their own bodies, belonged to the empire. Even if a contestant did not become queen, that did not mean she could then return home. Instead, she received a "consolation prize": she became part of the king's harem. But let us look more closely at this chapter.

The Establishment of the Rules of the Contest – 2:1–4

Now that Xerxes' anger had abated, his attendants must have felt a little sorry for him, so they proposed to him that a search covering the entire empire be made for "beautiful young virgins" (v. 2:2); young maidens then should be brought to the citadel at Shushan (Susa) for the king's assessment. Then, the proposal continued, these ladies should be placed under the care of Hegai, the king's eunuch and chief chamberlain, who oversaw the women. The girl who pleased the king would be made the new queen in place of Vashti.

The servants suggested three criteria for this prospective queen: beauty, youthfulness and virginity. All women who met these criteria were to be considered. These servants emphasized to the king the fact that these girls were to be "beautiful young virgins" by repeating this fact twice. The winner of this contest would be the woman who sexually pleased the king the most during their night with him as each girl's turn came up for a special night with him (v. 4).

The Introduction of the Contestant Named Esther – 2:5–7

We are surprised to not hear how the contest was going in the verses that immediately followed the introductory material in v. 1–4. Instead, the narrator interrupted the story momentarily to introduce a Jewish man named Mordecai. Another surprise was that he was living in the citadel of Shushan during the time of the Persian king named Ahasuerus, a.k.a. Xerxes, when the former king of the Medo-Persian empire, Cyrus the Great, had magnanimously declared 50 years before that the Jews could return to their homeland in Israel. Yet, here was a Jew, who had come from Jerusalem (v. 2:6), now living in the heart of this pagan nation's citadel! He did not choose to return with the 50,000 Jewish exiles that did, when the offer was made!

The name Mordecai was given to him as a local name patterned after the name of Marduk, a pagan god. This Hebrew form of the name was an attempt to bring into Hebrew the *marduka*, the Babylonian goddess of love. The author of this text intimated that Mordecai had some sort of connection with Saul, even if only indirect, through the fact that Mordecai was a "Benjamite," just as Saul was, and that Haman, the prime minster of Ahasuerus, was an Agagite, whom King Saul had been charged by the prophet Samuel to eradicate by the command of God (1 Sam. 15).

Mordecai, we also learn from 2:7, acts in this narrative as the adoptive parent for his cousin Esther. She also had the Hebrew name, *Hadassah*, meaning "myrtle," a fragrant shrub or tree. "Esther" is from the Persian word meaning "star," or "Ishtar," the Babylonian goddess of love. In Hebrew, this word sounds like the Hebrew for "I hide myself" or "I am hidden." Esther's mother and father were no longer living, so she was an orphan under Mordecai's care and upbringing.

Esther was noted for being "lovely in form and features" (v. 7b); that is why she was "good to look at" (*tovat mar'eh*) and "fair of form" (*yefatto'ar*). In her new role as one of the women selected for the beauty contest, Esther learned both how to survive and thrive in that foreign environment. First, she learned quickly how to "find favor" (*matsa' hen*) in the eyes of Hegai, the "keeper of the women." Thus, Esther will survive in this foreign culture! It will also stand her in good stead when she comes before King Xerxes.

Esther Wins the Contest but Hides Her Nationality – 2:8–16

As a result of the search throughout the empire, a good many girls were gathered (perhaps hundreds) and brought to the citadel. Esther was among those taken to the palace and entrusted to Hegai, for she was said to be placed "into the hand of" Hegai, the man responsible for providing the women with a year-long beauty treatment and with all the necessities they would need for their evening with the king (vv. 9, 12–14). Scripture does not say whether the women had any voice in their selection, or if they did not desire to be in the contest. Their will was of no interest to those who went out to conduct the search. However, each virgin was transported to the capital city of Shushan and placed in the care of Hegai the harem-keeper.

What troubles the believing reader of this story, however, is why there is there no outcry from the Jewish population in the empire against the demands that are made of these virgins? Why is it that neither Esther nor Mordecai raise any protest against marrying a heathen? Was there no concept of separation of the holy from the unholy at this time? Why does the text not record even one prayer from the main characters in this story, or a prayer from anyone of the Jewish people about this situation? Does this mean that the Jewish people at this point welcomed the prospect of Jewish assimilation to the Gentile unbelieving culture? It all seems so strange!

The only clue we are given is v. 9, where Esther "pleased" Hegai and "won his favor." Thus, he assigned her "seven maids" who "moved her ... into the best place in the harem" (v. 9b). Because of Esther's securing Hegai's good-will, he began her beauty regime, using the cosmetics and beauty-enhancing procedures, earlier than usual. Esther showed no resistance to the special treatment suggested for these maids. In doing so, she displayed an excellent attitude and one who had good interpersonal relations, not only with Hegai and these handmaids, but also with Mordecai.

It is not known if Esther requested that she be fed only kosher foods, just as Daniel and his friends had done (Dan. 1:8–16), for we are never told that Esther did not eat non-kosher foods during the twelve months of her beauty treatments. How compliant she was to the teachings of her faith?

There was one dark secret Mordecai had directed her not to disclose to anyone: her Jewish identity (v. 10). She showed no resistance to the obligation her cousin had placed on her not to reveal she was Jewish. Was this then a sign of the betrayal of both Esther and Mordecai to their heritage? Would this also be sign of their betrayal of their faith in God? We are told that Mordecai was deeply concerned for Esther, for day after day he walked back and forth in an area close to the harem, hoping, to catch a glimpse of his cousin (v. 11). He was concerned for Esther's well-being and her success as a contestant.

The exact formula for the year-long beauty treatment is given in vv. 12–14. The process involved four specific steps for all the women: (1) a year-long beautification treatment, (2) a night attempting to please the king sexually, on his request, (3) a transfer to a second harem chamber after the evening was over, and (4) a period of waiting to see if the king would summon her again to spend another night attempting to arouse him. When it came time for a woman to take her turn to go into bed with the king for the night, she was allowed to take anything she wished from the harem. Each woman's time would begin in the evening and end in the morning (v. 14), when she would then go to the care of Shashgaz, who oversaw the concubines. But when it came time for Esther's turn, she did not request to take anything other than that which Hegai had given her (v. 15).

And so it happened that "Esther won the favor of everyone who saw her" (v. 15c). She was taken to Xerxes at his royal residence in the tenth month, the month of Tebeth, in the seventh year of his reign (v. 16). This would be about four years after Queen Vashti had been deposed (1:10–21), after Xerxes' return from his Grecian campaign.

A Marriage Made in Shushan– 2:17–23

Verse 17 begins, "Now the king was attracted to Esther more than to any other woman, and she won his favor and approval more than any of the other virgins." The king made sure he set on Esther's head the crown that had once been on Vashti's head. Also, he threw a great banquet for all his nobles and officials as he announced a holiday throughout the empire. Added to this was his distribution of gifts backed by his royal generosity and liberality (v. 18).

One thing remained as previously: Esther kept the secret of her background and nationality a secret (v. 20). She remained faithful to the instructions that Mordecai had given now that she was in the palace, just as she did while she was growing up (v. 20c).

Meanwhile, all this time Mordecai continued to sit at the king's gate. Because he so often was there, Mordecai overheard Bigthana and Teresh, two of the king's officers who guarded the doorway to the citadel, plot in their anger to assassinate Xerxes (v. 22). When Mordecai learned what these insurrectionists planned to do, he related that information to Esther, who reported it to the king but gave full credit to Mordecai for the intelligence (v. 22). The king investigated and discovered it indeed was true, so the two royal officers were both hanged on the gallows (v. 23). All this was carefully recorded in the book of the annals of the king in his presence.

Some "creatively" interpret the scenes of the book of Esther as allegory, with the meanings of the text to be found in the values that are externally assigned to the characters and events in this book. However, there is little if any indication that these values and so-called "deeper meanings" were in this book. For example, Xerxes is autocratically said to represent the LORD of the Universe (ADONAI). Mordecai symbolizes Yeshua. The seven servants and the seven wise men are likewise said to represent executive and judicial powers in action. The seven maidens who helped Esther were said to symbolize the sevenfold Spirit of God (Isa. 11:2). Thus, just as Esther kept her Jewish identity secret, so the true identity of the Church, which is the Bride of Christ, is hidden from Israel! Esther, then, is a type of the Church, and Vashti is a type of Israel. Moreover, just as Esther was chosen, the Church has now also been chosen. Finally, the two royal guards typify two areas of man's being: his spiritual nature and his earthly nature. We mortals need guidance in both areas, but they also represent a conspiracy against God's Kingdom and his laws, and therefore they must be removed!

Wow! How do people teach such stuff with no authoritative backing from the words of Scripture?[1]

---

1. Frank J. Olsen, *The Mystery of Esther: God's Prophetic Plan*, 15–25.

Conclusions

1. Esther happened to be living in the capital of Persia because of the sin and disobedience of her forebearers that had brought the family of Mordecai and Esther into exile in the days of Judah's King Jehoiachin.

2. This disobedience had kept these families in exile, for King Cyrus had issued a decree permitting all Jews to return to their homeland in 538 B.C.E., yet neither Mordecai nor Esther had accepted this offer of freedom, which some 50,000 did.

3. Mordecai forced Esther to hide her nationality and faith, but she was not instructed to deny that faith! Moreover, the pressure to conform to the culture came from within her own family and not from the pagan empire.

4. We also learn that despite this disobedience to God, he alone can turn the bitter fruits of our parents' disobedience to his own glory and purposes.

5. God hovers over every single detail in our lives by moving the pieces into a coordinated plan that works out what he wants accomplished.

Questions for Thought and Reflection

1. Was God limited to Esther and the beauty pageant to get his work done, or could he also have done it another way? (See v. 4:14.)

2. If Vashti was already showing her baby late in her pregnancy, was she right in refusing to obey the king's command?

3. Did the Lord still condemn polygamy even for pagan kings?

4. Why does this Scripture attach this story to King Saul's failure years ago to eradicate all the Agagites? How does Haman play into this part of the story?

5. What can we gather from the story about Esther's character?

Lessons 3-4

Mordecai Takes a Stand and Urges Esther to Do Likewise

Esther 3:1–15; 4:1–17

Suddenly, for some unknown reason, Xerxes decided to honor Haman, a man in his government. But who was he, and what is an Agagite? To take the second question first, an Agagite was a person from the lineage of Agag, a king of the Amalekites, the descendants of Amalek; these tribes were mentioned in the line of Esau, Jacob's oldest son. Genesis 36:12 stated, "And Timna was a concubine to Eliphaz, Esau's son; and she bore to Eliphaz [one named] Amalek." Let us pick up the story before we get to this critical detail.

Five years seem to have elapsed since the two guards' intended coup, the plot Mordecai discovered and Esther related to the king. This narrative may have been deliberately understated to keep things from spreading, but suddenly Haman is seen exercising enormous powers of the empire in his "twelfth year" (v. 3:7). His advisers have suddenly disappeared from power, and in their place, Haman was the newly empowered officer with "a seat of honor higher than all the other nobles" (v. 3:1). Let's look at this text.

Mordecai Refuses to Bow to Haman – 3:1–5

We are introduced to Haman the Agagite immediately; he had just been promoted by Xerxes to prime minster. The king advanced him so far over the officers and nobles in his court that they all had to bow down and honor him, "for the king had commanded this" (v. 2). But in God's providence, it so happened that Haman's promotion came shortly after Mordecai got wind of the guards' plot, which he related through Esther to Xerxes and saved his life. But a protest against Mordecai broke out at about the same time, for the royal officials at the king's gate accused him of refusing to obey the command to bow down to those in the gate area (v. 3). Mordecai's behavior evidenced civil disobedience to the law of the king as well as a public affront to Persian law and order. Not only was Haman's honor at stake, but so was that of the rest of the officials and nobles (v. 3).

The people at the king's gate kept after Mordecai day after day to bow down as required, but he "did not listen to them." He just "refused to comply" (v. 4). He did attempt to explain why he refused to comply: "he told them he was a Jew" (v. 4b). His refusal was a matter of theological conviction! But in giving that explanation, he let slip that he had a Jewish background.

Xerxes' servants decided to test whether Mordecai's explanation would stand up, for his claim to being a Jew was a claim that he should be granted a religious exemption from the rule that he must bow before mortals. His religion forbade him! The guards chose to tell Haman, who up to this point had not noticed Mordecai's truculent behavior. However, once he heard this man was Jewish, there was no further need to persuade Haman. Was this an indication of a residual amount of antisemitism among their ranks, or could it be that some were angry because it was somehow known that Mordecai had told the king of Bigthana and Teresh's plot? This may have indicated a revolution afoot within the empire. Antisemitism may have been its fuel. We do not know for sure!

Up to this point, Mordecai had been hiding his Jewish identity for the same reason he had urged Esther to. Mordecai's divulgence of his identity came at the same time as his reporting the names of the two anarchists. Once the servants learned he was Jewish, they felt it was time to get this information out about his refusing to bow in acknowledgment of the king's command to the right people.

Why Haman was set off in a rage when he was told these facts is not entirely clear; apparently, he had not noticed anything amiss when he had previously passed through the king's gate (v. 5). He is described as using an extraordinarily strong word for his anger, *hamah*, which is used six times in Esther (four times of the king, vv. 1:12; 2:1; 7:7,10 and twice of Haman, 3:5; 5:9). Yes, there was the matter of Mordecai's public affront to his honor, but was the degree of his anger even greater because it might have entailed his deep antipathy to the Jews and an ethnic feud he had nursed from previous days?

Haman Calls for Vengeance on All Jews – 3:6–9

Once Haman found out Mordecai was a Jew, he was not satisfied with killing just him; he now sought a way to destroy all Jewish people in every part of Xerxes' kingdom (v. 6). Haman twice called the Jewish people the "people of Mordecai." Did some of this antipathy, however, go back to the ancient hostility that arose between King Saul the Benjaminite and the descendants of Agag, the king of the people from whom Haman was descended?

The Hebrew text of v. 7 boldly begins with the fact that on the "first month, the month of Nisan" (Lev. 16:8), it was decided to hold a lottery to determine when the dastardly deed of liquidating the Jewish people should take place. This was now Xerxes' "twelfth year," some five years after the events in chapter 2. But the month of Nisan was an especially pointed reminder of Israel's great deliverance from Egypt, when they had celebrated the Passover for the first time!

They cast the *pur*, the Persian word for the "lot," in Haman's presence, to select a day and month when this genocide should happen. The lot fell on the twelfth month, Adar. Such an act of casting lots was used in the Ancient Near East (Lev. 16:8; Jos. 15:1, 17:1; Judg. 20:9; Neh. 11:1); in fact, Proverbs 16:33 taught, "The lot is cast into the lap, but its every direction is from the LORD." The Septuagint added the exact day, "the thirteenth," which for some reason is missing from the Hebrew text, or perhaps the king left the exact day up to Haman. Certainly, Haman is represented as having unrestricted access to the king. Such access was not afforded to the rest of the people.

Haman promised that if King Xerxes approved his plan, he would enrich the national treasury of Persia by 10,000 talents of silver, which some scholars estimate is about 60% of the annual Persian revenue that could come into the coffers of the land (v. 9).

Haman's Plan Is Put into Action – 3:10–15

It is astounding how readily Xerxes accepted Haman's plan to remove the Jewish people for the empire (v. 10). The king handed over to him the authorizing seal of his government via his signet ring, using his full name, "Haman son of Hammadatha, the Agagite, the enemy of the Jews." The reference to the "enemy of the Jews" is an extraordinarily strong term, for it literally reads "one who hates the Jews" (*soneh*). The king tells him to "keep his money," but "do with the people as you please" (v. 11). Now in this text, the "thirteenth day" is specified (v. 12), the day before Passover, when Israel gained their freedom for Egypt. But this time it would not be another day of deliverance but a day of annihilation from another foreign government!

The royal secretaries were summoned to write anything and everything Haman ordered, which these scribes posted all over the empire for all the provinces to read. Then couriers were dispatched throughout the empire to carry the sad news, which it certainly was for the people of Israel. Meanwhile, King Xerxes and Haman sat down to drink while the city of Shushan was tremendously bewildered as to the meaning of all of this (v. 15).

The Jewish Community Is Thrown into Deep Mourning – 4:1–3

Mordecai was first to learn of this new legislative development, for the gossip and intelligence network in the king's gate must have been up on all such new developments (4:1). This Jewish man tore his clothes and put on sackcloth and ashes on his head (the sign of deep mourning) and went out into the city, wailing as loudly and bitterly as he could. What Mordecai now wore was sackcloth made of goat or camelhair, the traditional Jewish expression of self-humiliation. Surely, he felt partly responsible for what had befallen his people. Even his use of the "dust and ashes" symbolized ritual impurity and separation from God.

The fourth chapter may be the best expression of spirituality in the Book of Esther. "In every province" of the empire, the Jews met the announcement of their coming doom "with fasting, weeping and wailing" (v. 3). It is not at all insignificant that the people, using the same Hebrew terms, do what the Lord declared through the prophet Joel that a backsliding and rebellious Israel should do in their situation as well: "Return to me with all your heart, with fasting (*tsom*), with weeping (*bakah*), and with wailing (*sapad*) (Joel 2:12). However, the one term missing in Esther from the four terms in Joel 2:12 was (*teshuvah*)—there was no indication that the people "returned" to the Lord. Moreover, the people in Esther tore their clothes, but Joel 2:13 went on to call those who sought a genuine revival also to tear their hearts, not just their clothes.

Mordecai Challenges Esther and She Responds – 4:4–17

Esther's maids and eunuchs broke the news to her about Mordecai, which naturally brought her great distress (v. 4). Apparently, she did not fully understand all that was going on, so to relieve the embarrassment of her cousin going through the city of Shushan weeping and wailing, tearing his clothes in deep grief, Esther sent clothing to Mordecai to replace the sackcloth she heard he had donned, hoping that would calm his outbursts, but he refused to accept them (v. 4c). Esther was determined to get to the bottom of what was going on, so she sent a eunuch named Hathach, who had already been assigned to help her, with orders to find out what had so upset Mordecai. (Hebrew uses the interrogative, *mah-zeh*, asking: "Why did this happen?")

Hathach located Mordecai in the open square of the city in front of the king's gate (v. 6). Mordecai told him all that had happened, including the edict to bow before Haman, his deep revulsion, and his commitment as a Jew not to. He also told Hathach that Haman had offered 10,000 talents into the royal treasury to pay for the destruction of the Jews (v. 7). Mordecai gave Hathach a copy of the edict for the

Jewish annihilation, which by this time had been published in the capital city of Susa, to the Jews' horror, in case she had any doubts about the reality of this story (v. 8).

Mordecai then asked Hathach to urge Esther to go personally into the presence of the king "to beg for mercy and to plead with him for her people" (v. 8c). All this Hathach faithfully brought to Esther (v. 9). No longer was Mordecai holding Esther responsible for hiding her identity as a Jew, for now he wanted her to disclose that fact before Xerxes.

But Esther felt as if Mordecai had forgotten how serious it was for someone in the court to unceremoniously appear before the king without being summoned. So, she sent Hathach back to Mordecai with the reminder that for her to do what her cousin was advocating could mean certain death for her (v. 11). Thus, she expressed a reluctance to do what Mordecai was urging her to do. This "no-approach policy" of the Persian court was well-known (e.g., Herodotus 1.99; 3.77–84). Yes, there were occasional exceptions, for one could make an appeal for such an audience (Herodotus 3.140), but how could a woman use this method when she had no recourse to a messenger, such as the men had? Moreover, it had been 30 days since Esther had been called to go before the king. How could she or they count on such a fortuitous day appearing suddenly in the future?

When Hathach repeated Esther's words, Mordecai emphatically urged him to return to Esther and tell her she was not to assume that just because she was in the king's house that she alone, of all the Jews, would escape the coming genocide (v. 12). Her privileged position would be just as vulnerable as that of any other Jew. Once Haman discovered that she too was a Jew and that she was also related to Mordecai, she would be killed as far as he was concerned. Mordecai may also have been hinting that if deliverance had to come from some other source due to Esther's intransigence and unwillingness to risk putting herself in harm's way, then she could expect harm to come to her from the Jews themselves, as they too might take out their frustration on her (v. 14)!

Mordecai, though, evidenced a strong confidence in God's unwavering providence, which he spoke by circumlocution— "relief and deliverance ... will arise from another place" (v. 14). The One who had been left unnamed in this narrative but was understood to be fully at work behind the scenes was the living God. She, in God's providence, had been placed in the position she now held by the unseen hand of providence. This could be her moment and the moment for which she had been born. She may "have come to [the kingdom] for such a time as this" (v. 14). She had to act!

Mordecai's message had gotten through, for Esther sent back the reply he was hoping for! However, if she were going to undertake this mission, Mordecai must go and gather all the Jews in Susa to "fast for [her], refuse to eat or drink anything for three days and nights, which Esther and her maids would also practice during that same time (vv. 15–16). When the three days were up, she would gather her courage and go to the king even though it was against the law. "If [she] perished, [she] perished" (v. 16). Mordecai left and carried out the instructions given him by Esther. Now in this moment of extreme crisis, Esther had chosen to identify with her people even though it might cost her very life!

Conclusions

1. Mordecai evidenced at least part of his religious convictions when he refused to bow down to another mortal.

2. The casting of the "lot," called in Persian the *pur*, seemed to be a routine matter even to the choice of the day it was cast and its implication for the history of Israel.

3. Mordecai publicly demonstrated his deep grief over this decree to kill him and all his fellow Jews, which became the basis for arousing Esther into action as well.

4. Esther tried to send clothes for Mordecai to wear instead of sackcloth, but he would not be deterred from his mission to alert Esther and all Jews to the seriousness of the problem at hand!

5. Mordecai warned Esther that if she remained silent over what was happening, relief might have to come to the people of Israel from some other direction, but she should surely know that she herself had come to be queen of the empire at this vital time (4:14).

Questions for Thought and Reflection

1. Why does the text keep emphasizing that Haman was an Agagite? What may be behind this retention of an old score that Haman felt had to be resolved by him?

2. Why was kneeling and paying honor to another person seen to be so wrong for Mordecai? Would it also be wrong for us today to kneel before another person in honor of them?

3. Why did Xerxes hand over his ceremonial ring to Haman to use? Was this a way of the king's absolving himself of direct blame in the liquidation of the Jewish people?

4. Once the nation found out that Mordecai was related to Esther, would not his actions of wearing sackcloth and going about the city wailing and mourning bring discredit to the new queen?

5. How many instances of the quiet providence of God can you see in this story of Esther up to this point. How many other instances of divine providence, both scriptural and secular, can you cite as parallels to God's work in this story?

6. What is so wrong about being an antisemite, and why is it so prevalent in the world? What has given rise to it?

Lessons 5–7

Queen Esther Invites King Xerxes and Haman to Two Banquets

Esther 5:1–14, 7:8

Esther Makes Her Move – 5:1–2

As instructed by Mordecai, Queen Esther prepared to enter the king's presence without being summoned, even though it was against the law to barge in that way! Her only request of Mordecai was to gather all the Jews in Susa and fast for her during the next three days and nights. Esther and her maids would do the same, for she was now determined to go before the king unsummoned; she had concluded, "If I perish, I perish" (4:16).

Esther clothed herself in her new royal attire (*malkut*), for she had planned to enter the king's presence not just dressed up but to be on his footing and winsomely attractive. She stood waiting to be noticed while the king sat (5:1) on his throne in the "king's hall," which faced the entrance to the palace. Persian culture dictated that there was to be a separation between the majesty and dignity of the king and all his subjects, but now Esther had crossed the threshold of the entrance to the king's hall into the sacred space. There was no turning back now. Esther had to continue her quest, come what may!

The lingering question was, how had the fasting of so many gone? Had it paid off? In biblical times, fasting was one of the main ways of expressing contrition for sins or to show dependence on God in the face of calamity or tragedy—both on a personal and national level! Fasting was also a statement that there was more to life than mere physical existence. Life was not to be summed up as "Eat, drink and be merry, for tomorrow we die." Even today, fasting is an appropriate response to problems, personal or corporate (Deut. 9:18; Ezra 10:6; Neh. 1:4).

This does not mean that fasting and abstaining was a method of gaining God's attention. Such fasting also involved heartfelt prayers and a life obedient to the teachings of Scripture. So why is fasting seen so seldomly in our day? Are we too comfortable with our world as it is, or are we too proud to humble ourselves in that manner? Even in Esther's day, people did not fast until things began to be too complex and threatening for them. Even Esther had more to do than merely fast, for if she were not willing to go in before the king to make her request known to him, it would be without effect!

Mercifully, when Xerxes saw his queen standing in the court foyer, he was pleased with her and held out the merciful symbol of "favor," the gold scepter. Esther, no doubt with her heart in her hands, proceeded to approach the king and touch the tip of the scepter (v. 5:2). Now, let's witness the central action of this book.

Esther Invites King Xerxes and Haman to a Banquet – 5:3–8

The king saw that something troubled Esther—something great enough that she would risk her life to enter his presence, as she broke court protocol to go to him. So, Xerxes probed Esther about what was bothering her (v. 3). In fact, in what sounded like conventional royal response, he promised he was willing to assuage her anxieties with anything "up to half the kingdom" (v. 3b). This king had already extended the scepter that guaranteed Esther her life, and now he promised her part ownership of the kingdom. That should have put her heart and mind at ease, at least for the moment!

But Esther was a woman of careful strategy, for she made what might have seemed a rather mild request: Could the king and Haman come to a banquet today, one she had specially prepared for them? (v. 4) But the king was wise enough to know there was more than just an invitation going on; after he sent for Haman to come to the court, the king was set to hear Esther's request. But this little party later relaxed as they drank wine together (usually a separate course for drinking wine would come toward the end of the meal), and Xerxes thought it time for Esther to tell what it was she wanted (v. 6). To be sure, the venue of a private banquet would provide a more secluded area for her to make her request, given its delicate nature.

Without even hinting at the nature of her request, she carefully worded the exact way she wanted the men to come to a second banquet on the next day (v. 8). She said, "Let the king come [singular form] and Haman." They were not addressed together in the plural form of the verb. She gave no more hints than that precise wording of her invitation—that was all! If the men would accede to her request, she would answer the king's question (v. 8d).

Haman Gets Counsel from His Wife Zeresh – 5:9–14

Haman left the palace court happy as a lark, filled with "joy" and "high spirits" (v. 9)—that is, until he saw his nemesis Mordecai once again at the king's gate. Ever since Xerxes had learned that Mordecai refused to bow to him, he was more than just miffed; he was "filled with rage against Mordecai" (v. 9). Mordecai neither rose to stand, nor did he show any fear of Haman's presence, prestige, or power! However, at least on this occasion, Haman restrained himself and went home distraught (v. 10).

Haman called his friends together, no doubt boasting about his wealth, the number of sons his wife had given him, and now the way the king had singled him out for the distinct honor of dining with the king and queen, effectively setting him above every other noble and official in the Persian Empire (v. 11)! Of course, these nobles had heard all this before; it is clear Haman was a real braggard and proud beyond measure! But they had not heard about the banquet before, for this was his latest achievement. He wanted to make sure his friends got the point: He was the "only person" invited to these banquets (v. 12a).

However, Haman confessed that all of this, thrilling as it may have been, was lost on him "as long as that Jew Mordecai [was] sitting at the king's gate" (v. 13b). Two royal banquets right in a row, one after the other, and he still was not content, for quite frankly, this Jewish man had stolen his joy and ruined his day for him!

It seemed everyone in Persia had an adviser, and so it was with Haman. However, his wife Zeresh took the lead in offering advice (v. 14), which Haman's friends seemed to approve, to "have gallows built, seventy-five feet high, and ask the king in the morning to have Mordecai hanged on it. Then go with the king to the dinner and be happy" (v. 14b). The height of the gallows was crafted so outrageously tall, likely so it could be seen all over Susa. His counselors urged that Mordecai be impaled on this tall pole, to indicate the height of Haman's fury. Haman's advisors may have intended some irony here, for the man who would not bow to their friend Haman would rise to look on his house from 75 feet above! With that deed accomplished, thanks to his wife Zeresh's idea, Haman could go to his banquet joyfully, filled with a real sense of victory over the one who had drained him of any pleasure in life.

Sleepless Xerxes Discovers Mordecai Was Never Rewarded – 6:1–3

On the very night these plans were set, the king had a wretchedly sleepless night. He was deeply troubled, but he did not know why. Was he, the king, apprehensive about what Esther might ask him? And why had she insisted that Haman also be there? Was something bad about to happen to his kingship? That question may have been dimly raised in his mind, but he still could not bring it up to his consciousness.

One remedy he often resorted to for such loss of sleep was reading "the book of remembrances." When it was brought and read to him by court readers, who no doubt droned on for a long time that night, suddenly it was found that a man named Mordecai told the king and the palace that two men, Bigthana and Teresh, who guarded the doorway to the palace, had conspired against Xerxes to assassinate him (v. 2). He asked, "What honor and recognition has Mordecai received for this?" The attendant answered, "Nothing has been done for him" (v. 3). All of this could not have been more precisely timed, for things began to happen by the minute as history changed and so did things in the empire based on this reading of a dull record. The king may have been more worried about his own shame over leaving such a major issue unrewarded and unattended to, especially as it concerned his own well-being. This had to be fixed immediately!

Haman Thinks the King Wants to Honor Him – 6:4–9

Eventually the king asked, during the reading of the kingdom's official chronicles, if anyone happened to be in the court at that early moment in the morning. Guess who stepped forward: our wealthy and honorable official Haman; he had just stepped into the outer court of the palace, for he had some extremely important business he needed the king's permission to act on (v. 4). Talk about providential timing; how much timelier could such an event be!

Apparently, neither the king nor Haman had slept much. Both, for different reasons, had Mordecai on their minds, so sleep was totally unavailable! Haman was quite confident he was in the king's good graces, so he arrived earlier than on previous days to seem like he cared for his concerns. He had a matter about which he wanted the king's immediate approval: could he publicly hang Mordecai for his insubordination? But the king beat him to the punch by asking his own question, one that knocked Haman off his props completely: "What should be done for the man the king delights to honor?" (v. 6)

That was not a hard question for Haman, for certainly the king must have been thinking of no one other than himself, he reasoned! So, he fired off just what he wanted to see the king do for his faithful servant Haman:

> "For the man the king delights to honor, have them bring a royal
> robe the king has worn and a horse the king has ridden, one with
> a royal crest placed on its head. Then let the robe and the horse
> be entrusted to one of the king's noble princes. Let him robe the
> man he delights to honor and lead him on the horse through the
> city streets, proclaiming before him, 'This is what is done for the
> man the king delights to honor.'" (6:7–9)

Haman must have been thrilled with the king's repetition of the clause "the man whom the king delights to honor." Who else could the king be referring to? Haman was brimming with an inordinate amount of pride! Moreover, he clearly had designs on royal sovereign power, for the robe had to have been worn by the king, and the horse must have been ridden on by the king. Could it have been that as a result of the previous night's ruminations, the king was beginning to smell a rat as he considered Haman's past actions with a slight amount of suspicion. Also, Haman wanted the horse to wear on its head the royal crest, which was not an unusual headpiece for animals in the royal retinue. Haman's mighty-high opinion of himself knew few, if any, bounds.

Zeresh Predicts Her Husband Haman Will Come to Ruin – 6:10–13

What Haman heard next must have hit like a ton of bricks: "Go at once. … Get the robe and the horse and do just as you have suggested for Mordecai the Jew, who sits at the king's gate. Do not neglect anything you have recommended" (v. 10). When the king dropped Mordecai's despised name, we can only imagine the expression on Haman's face. How did the king know Mordecai was Jewish? Had that been written also into the chronicles? How could Xerxes not have known all Jews in his empire had been consigned to destruction? Had he forgotten or never read the mandate he signed at Haman's bidding? With the pending onslaught of the Jewish people, how does his desire to honor Mordecai factor into all of what was happening? Is he as ruler unaware of the developing antisemitic attitudes that were growing in his empire? Regardless of the answers, his parting shot to Haman made clear that Haman was to follow to the letter all that he had prescribed for this one, named Mordecai, whom the king wanted to honor. Anyone who had saved your neck was worthy of the most exacting honors one could give, and Haman was not to neglect anything he had described!

There is no record of what Mordecai thought about all of this. Surely his number one nemesis had tried to favor himself so extravagantly that it must have shocked him! Haman finished his humiliating ordeal as quickly as possible and fled home with his head covered in grief (v. 12). Once again, his wife Zeresh appeared as his chief adviser and counselor, followed by other advisers. Their advice was not too cheery; in fact, it was downright disheartening. Verse 13b:

> "Since Mordecai, before whom your downfall has started, is of Jewish origin, you cannot stand against him—you will surely come to ruin."

Note that Haman's advisers are no longer called his "friends;" they realized his doom was sealed, and he was on his way out in the government! There is a rabbinic expansion that has Haman's daughter watching the procession her father is leading through the streets of Susa, but since she did not recognize her father, she emptied a chamber-pot on him, thinking he was Haman. When she discovered her mistake, she threw herself to the ground and killed herself. As Haman hurried home from his impromptu parade, he might also have mourned for his daughter, an added burden to his grief.

At a Second Banquet Esther Asks the King to Spare Her Life and the Lives of Her People – 6:14–7:8

The agonizing discussion and repeated rehearsal of what had happened on that fateful day to the house of Haman continued as the king's eunuchs arrived to escort him to the queen's second banquet (v. 14). This was court protocol for those who had the standing in government Haman had attained. As these escorts arrived, they found their guest of honor during a conversation that entangled the lives of the whole family. But they hurried Haman away as quickly as they could. So, the king and Haman went to dinner together at Queen Esther's request. But as they were drinking wine again on the second day, Xerxes asked the same question now the third time, for by now he must have been most anxious to hear what was bothering her that she had made such careful plans for these dinners.

Moreover, for the second time, Xerxes promised to give Esther up to half of the empire. Esther was now ready to talk.

Cautiously she began by saying,

"If I have found favor with you, O king, and if it pleases your majesty to grant me my life—this is my petition. And spare my people—this is my request. For I and my people have been sold for destruction and slaughter and annihilation. If we had merely been sold as male and female slaves, I would have kept quiet, because no such distress would justify disturbing the king." (7:3–4)

Immediately King Xerxes demanded, "Who is he? Where is the man who has dared to do such a thing?" In the original Hebrew, the king repeats "said" twice, which indicates he had started sputtering as he was so taken back by Esther's new disclosure.

Esther did not hesitate, sensing she had suddenly gained the initiative, for she must have pointed at Haman as she announced: "The adversary and enemy is this vile Haman." Talk about having a dreadful day—Haman must have thought the entire world was collapsing on him suddenly. And it was!

Naturally, he was "terrified," but the king flew into a rage as he suddenly got up and left to go into the palace garden. Haman now knew he was in deep trouble with the king, for he must also have sensed the king had already decided his fate. To make matters worse, he stayed behind to plead with Esther for his life. As the king stormed back into the banquet room, he caught Haman falling over the couch on which Esther was reclining. That settled the whole matter: The king yelled, "Will you even molest the queen while she is with me in the house?" (v. 8b) No sooner had Xerxes said this than his servants covered Haman's face. He was a dead man for sure!

It was Harbona, a eunuch, who commented to the king, "A gallows seventy-five feet high stands by Haman's house. He had made it for Mordecai, who spoke up to help the king" (v. 9). What irony, that the gallows that had been built to hang the man Haman hated turned out to be the structure on which Haman himself would be hanged! Harbona cleverly gave the king a second reason to execute: Haman had planned to use those very gallows to hang Mordecai after he helped foil the plot on Xerxes' life! This surely helped Harbona's status with the king as well.

Conclusions

1. After three days of fasting and prayer, Esther donned her royal robes and approached the king's hall, knowing she might die for this act: "If I perish, I perish."

2. Mercifully, King Xerxes held out his gold scepter and invited Esther to touch its tip and enter the king's presence.

3. Esther decided to invite the king and Haman to banquets on two successive days, where she would make her request of the king.

4. In the meantime, the king caught up on his required reading of the chronicles of the kingdom, only to find out nothing had been done to thank Mordecai for alerting him and his empire to a planned coup that had since been discovered and foiled.

5. Haman, supposing he was the man the king wanted to honor, laid out an elaborate parade through the streets of Susa for that person clothed in a royal robe and royal horse, only to find out it all was not for him, but for his nemesis, Mordecai.

Questions for Thought and Reflection

1. Do you think that Esther or Mordecai, as Jewish people, had any appreciation for the doctrine of Providence or even thought of it applying to them? Did it ever strike them at all?

2. How did Esther summon the courage to face Haman directly as she dramatically pointed to him and accused him of issuing a death sentence to her and her people?

3. By placing the banquets on two successive days, do you think Esther deliberately increased the drama and explosiveness of the charge she would make against Haman?

4. Do you detect a smile on Esther's face as it turned out the person who happened to be in the court waiting room that early morning was none other than Haman? Did that surprise start to open her up to the fact that God was still in charge and had not forgotten his people, Israel?

5. Many of Haman's neighbors must have asked him why he was building such high gallows, only to be stunned to later see him leading Mordecai through the streets with such praise coming from the man they had just heard condemn Mordecai to death–he was now honored. What do you think?

Lessons 8–10

Esther's Appeal for
Justice and Vengeance

Esther 8:1–10:3

Finally, King Xerxes learned that Esther was related to Mordecai. Considering this family relationship, and the fact that the king had just learned that Mordecai was the one who foiled the plot on the king's life, Xerxes removed his royal signet ring, which he had just reclaimed from the hanged Haman's hand and presented it to Mordecai. Moreover, he deeded to Esther Haman's total estate (v. 1–2).

Now for the second time, Esther found it her job once again to go unannounced to beg Xerxes to allow the Jewish people to protect themselves and to assemble in every city to right the wrongs that had been committed against her people.

Armed forces of any nationality or province that might attack them for being Jewish, including their women or children (vv. 3, 11), were at risk of destruction.

Esther fell at the king's feet, weeping, begging him to let the Jewish people defend themselves against the treacherous plan Haman the Agagite had instituted against them. Thus, Esther appears to have stood outside the court, once more awaiting the signal of his approval for her to enter his presence by extending his golden scepter. The signal came, and she entered the king's court and stood before him (v. 4).

When she had entered the royal chamber, Esther made her plea:

"If it pleases the king, and if he regards me with favor and thinks
it is the right thing to do, and if he is pleased with me, let an order
be written overruling the dispatches that Haman son of

> Hammedatha, the Agagite, devised and wrote to destroy the Jews in all the king's provinces. For how can I bear to see disaster fall on my people? How can I bear to see the destruction of my family?" (vv. 8:5–6)

In her address, Esther used a long preamble. Two clauses dealt with whether this matter was acceptable to the king; two dealt with whether she herself as queen was acceptable to him. The only reason he might oblige her request was his favorable response to her, for Esther made no reference to any issues of what was right or wrong, or just or unjust.

By this time the king had given Mordecai his signet ring, which carried imperial authority of the king; still, Mordecai did not immediately assert his own authority to approach the king on behalf of this action. Perhaps it was because of his high regard for Esther and her continuing relationship to the king that he held back from taking this action on his own and let Esther take the lead in formulating the request. Now that he wore the signet ring, Mordecai's power was second only to that of King Xerxes; nevertheless, both Mordecai and Esther were incredibly careful to observe the proper decorum in addressing the king and to make sure he was properly honored.

The king responded to Esther and Mordecai (v. 8:7), for Mordecai must have somehow by now have joined Esther on her second foray into the king's presence in the royal court, where the king asked both Esther and Mordecai to witness his directing another decree to be written in his name. The announcement read:

> Because Haman attacked the Jews, I have given his estate to Esther, and they have hanged him on the gallows. Now write another decree in the king's name on behalf of the Jews as seems best to you, and seal it with the king's signet ring—for no document written in the king's name and sealed with his ring can be revoked. (vv. 8:7–8)

Xerxes's statement is difficult to sort out, for he might have implied by this statement to Esther something like, "Look, I've already given an edit for making possible your fighting and taking defensive action, all of which is to be carried out in my empire in my name for one whole day—what else do you want!" Or he may have been in a more expansive mood in which his words implied, "I took care of Haman and his request; now you are free to do whatever else you want." Without knowing his tone of voice, facial expression, or gestures, it is not possible to make a definitive judgment.

The royal secretaries were summarily called for immediate action on the twenty-third day of the month of Sivan; thus, they wrote 70 days after the first edict had been completed (v. 9). But it was Mordecai who dictated the contents and substance of this edict, which was to be sent out to all Jews and to all satraps, governors, and nobles in all 127 provinces that extended from India to Cush. This edict provided for Jews in every city of the empire from India to Ethiopia to defend themselves and to kill, murder, and annihilate all the attackers who wanted to kill any of them (v. 8:11). The Jewish people were mercifully given the right to "avenge" themselves (v. 13b). The royal couriers took down the decree and put it into every language used within the empire. Then with the aid of the fastest horses in the empire, couriers sped across the miles on steeds that were reserved for imperial postage usage (v. 8:14).

The Use of Vengeance in Esther

What troubles Believers more than anything else in this book is the clause that gave the Jews the authority "to avenge themselves of their enemies." But several important distinctions are in order here if we are to properly understand this term "to avenge." The Hebrew root *naqam* is used in both its verbal and nominal forms with the warning that God's people were prevented from using this form of retaliation (i.e., taking vengeance) on their own. The Bible teaches that vengeance belonged exclusively to the Lord and not to any mortal (Lev. 19:18; Judg. 16:28). In most cases in Scripture, God is the One who exercises "vengeance" (Nah. 1:2; Lev. 26:25; Isa. 1:24; 34:8). There is no question that the crime Haman perpetrated on the Jewish people was terribly heinous, both because it called for the extinction of the Jews and because its effects have continued long after his death until this day, but that gave no grounds for personal vendetta!

The picture the prophet Nahum paints in Nahum 1:2–11 is that God is very zealous for his name and his cause, for all sin is an assault on his holiness and it is a defilement of all he is, and all he stands for (v. 1:2). Even though the Lord may withhold his wrath, even if it is for what seems like a long time, since he is the One who is slow to anger (v. 1:3). Nevertheless, "he will not leave the guilty unpunished" (v. 1:3b). He has set a time when he will judge the sins of the wicked (1 Pet. 2:9), for of this all persons can be certain.

Mordecai left the palace dressed in royal garments of white and blue, a large golden crown, and a purple robe of fine linen (v. 8:15). The colors of white and blue would be featured prominently in the Jewish prayer shawl as well as on the flag of Israel. But for the Jews all over the empire, it was a time of great happiness and joy, marked by feasting and celebration (vv. 16–17). In fact, many other peoples who became Jews because "the fear of the Jews seized them" (v. 17b).

Hopes of Overpowering the Jews Is Overturned – 9:1–10

Accordingly, on the thirteenth day of the month of Adar, the enemies of the Jews were completely overpowered throughout the empire, as the tables were sharply turned against them! The Jewish defenders easily gained the upper hand over those who had previously poured out hatred on them. God did not intervene by directly making waste and voiding Haman's decree. Instead, God turned the tables on the enemies of the Jews so radically that they never knew what hit them. The fact of the matter was, "No one could stand against the Jews" (v. 9:2). This suggests they had taken an offensive action against their enemies. People of all nationalities were frightened of the Jews as a real horror fell on the non-Jewish population. Xerxes had given the Jewish people the right to organize themselves to "stand for their lives" (vv. 8:11; 9:2). Moreover, the nobles of the provinces, the satraps, and the governors and king's administrators helped the Jews, simply because they suddenly became afraid of what Mordecai might do to them (v. 9:3), for Mordecai's reputation quickly spread all over the provinces of the empire, as he became more and more powerful (v. 4).

The Jewish response to those who had hated them and were intent on killing them was to wield their swords against them as they did what they pleased, considering the planned extinction they now faced (v. 9:5). In the capital city of Susa, the Jews killed 500 men, plus the ten sons of Haman, the Agagite and enemy of the Jews. Surprisingly, the Jews did not touch one bit of the plunder left by their enemies (vv. 7–10).

Esther Asks the King for an Additional Day to Defend Themselves in Susa – 9:11–17

King Xerxes was given a fatality report of the number of men who had been vanquished in Susa (v. 11). He then reported this number to Esther, while also prominently mentioning that along with that number the death of Haman's sons should be added (v. 12). But the king further questioned Esther, "What have they done to the rest of the king's provinces?" Since he addressed the question to Esther, he must have wondered what the Jews had done elsewhere in the kingdom, since 500 men had been lost in Susa (v. 12). Or did "they" refer to the enemies of the Jews and what sort of havoc they had done?

It may just as well have been a question to the forces of adversity, for in their attempt to carry out Haman's earlier decree, there is no doubt this was because of the confrontation of the two forces the spectacle of mayhem everywhere, with looting and fires throughout the kingdom. Considering all that, the king wanted to know from Esther if she had any additional petition to ask of him, or had things gone far enough (v. 12b). As it turned out, Esther did have one more request:

"Give the Jews in Susa permission to carry out this day's edict tomorrow and let Haman's ten sons be hanged on gallows." (9:13)

The king acquiesced to the request with permission of an additional day to retaliate in the capital city of Susa and that Haman's sons should be hanged (v. 14). Accordingly, 300 more men in Susa were added to the previous day's 500. However, once again, the Jews steadfastly refused to lay their hands on any of the enemy's plunder that had resulted from the battle (v. 15). The number of those killed in the rest of the provinces finally came in at a whopping 75,000, yet once again, there was no looting or taking of any plunder on the part of the Jews (v. 16). All this happened on the thirteenth and fourteenth days of the month of Adar, for then the Jewish population rested and declared these days to be days of feasting and joy (v. 17).

A Decree to Annually Celebrate This Victory – 9:18–32

The enemies of the Jews were soundly defeated as the Jewish people were rescued from destruction. Esther had moved with boldness and a show of courage and power given to her by the God who had from the beginning chosen to use Israel as the center of his plans. Thus, the Jews assembled on the fourteenth day in the rural villages, and on the fifteenth day in Susa set aside as a day of resting, feasting and joy (v. 9:18).

Mordecai recorded all these events and sent letters to all the Jews throughout the empire to set aside these two days, called Purim, to observe the miracle of deliverance they had just experienced (v. 20). Archaeologists have discovered Persian dice inscribed with *pur*, a "lot." These days were to celebrate the times when the Jewish people got relief from their enemies and when their sorrow was turned into joy and their mourning into celebration (v. 22). Mordecai wrote to the Jews so they would celebrate these as days not only of feasting and rejoicing but also of giving presents of food to one another and gifts to the poor (v. 22b).

Mordecai skillfully related the narrative they all had lived through while carefully avoiding placing any guilt or responsibility on King Xerxes. He also was careful to avoid emphasizing references to the parts that he or Esther had played so as not to detract attention from Xerxes. This restored to the king any tarnished honor he may have lost by his failure to stand up for the people in his kingdom!

Therefore, Mordecai told the story in a compressed form that began with Haman the Agagite casting the *pur* to determine the day set by casting the dies when the destruction of the Jewish people would take place. However, when Haman's plot came to the king's attention, Mordecai gently glossed it over by saying Xerxes gave written orders that the evil, which Haman had devised against the Jews, should fall back on his own head and that Haman and his sons should be hanged on the gallows. This is how these days, Mordecai taught, came to be called Purim, from the Persian word *pur* (vv. 24–26a). The Jews themselves made it a custom that they and their descendants would always observe these two days each year in the way Mordecai had outlined (vv. 27–28).

Along with Mordecai, Queen Esther, daughter of Abihail, wrote this second letter with the king's full authority concerning the feast of Purim. These letters were sent to all Jews in all 127 provinces of Xerxes' sphere, complete with words of good will and assurance (vv. 29–30). Thus, what was also known as Esther's decree, these regulations for the days of Purim, were entered into the book of records in Media and Persia.

An Inscription Is Placed in a Book of the Annals of the Kings of Medea and Persia – 10:1–3

These final three verses are not written in the "A-Text" of Esther and are thus designated as part of the additions made to this book. However, they do function well in bringing closure to the narrative of Esther in that they bring us full circle back to where the story began with the magnificence of Xerxes' realm and the scope of his power. This way, some space is provided for a recognition of the magnitude of Xerxes's rule and reign and without focusing solely on the praise for Esther and Mordecai. There is no doubt, though, of the stature Mordecai had achieved throughout the ordeal. He was greatly esteemed from that time on by his fellow Jews as he worked continuously for the "good of his people and spoke up for the welfare of all the Jews" (v. 10:3).

Conclusion

1. The signet ring that the king had stripped from Haman's hand was given to Mordecai to put on his finger. This providentially provided for the people of Israel in ways that Israel could not have dreamed possible.

2. Mordecai let Esther take the lead in pleading with the king to allow the Jews to defend themselves on the day of attack set by Haman.

3. The king's edict was granted to Esther. Therefore, Xerxes' couriers rode throughout the empire on the royal steeds to make sure all were informed of this action.

4. The Jews struck down their enemies in an overwhelming one- or two-day period of slaughter of over 75,000 men.

5. The fourteenth and fifteenth days of the month of Adar were set aside in the Jewish calendar to remember what had occurred in that time.

Questions for Thought and Reflection

1. Did the book of Esther permit the Jewish people to exercise personal vendetta and vengeance against their enemies? What Jewish teaching prevented this action, and where is it found?

2. Was Mordecai correct in urging his cousin Esther not to reveal her ethnic roots? What does this tell us about how deeply the culture of that empire was infected with anti-Semitism?

3. Why do you think that the king included the ten sons of Haman in the list of those who should be killed?

4. Suggest key places in this narrative where the silent and quiet hand of God's providence was operative even though it is not spelled out directly.

5. Why did many in the domain of Xerxes become Jewish? Did this mean they also converted to Judaism? Is fear a good prompter when moving to a new religious conviction?

Printed in the United States
by Baker & Taylor Publisher Services